The Donna Reed Show

THE
DONNA REED SHOW

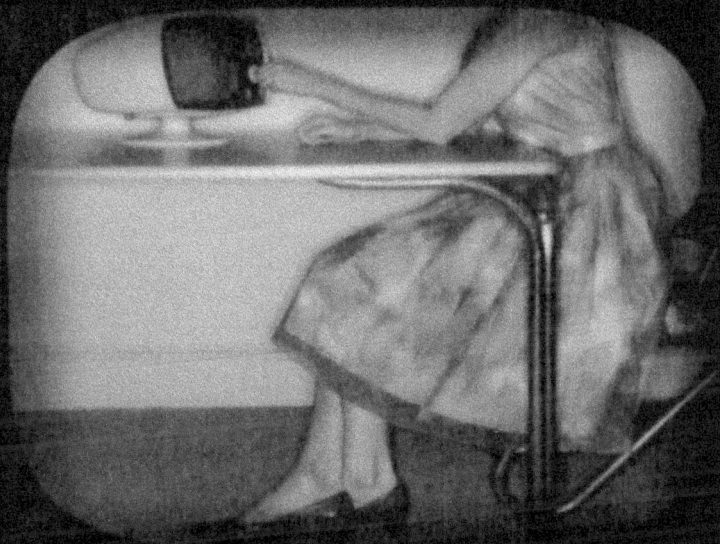

Joanne Morreale

TV MILESTONES SERIES

Wayne State University Press   Detroit

16 15 14 13 12   5 4 3 2 1

Library of Congress Cataloging-in-Publication Data

Morreale, Joanne, 1956–
The Donna Reed show / Joanne Morreale.
p. cm. — (Contemporary approaches to film and media series)
Includes bibliographical references and index.
ISBN 978-0-8143-3508-6 (pbk. : alk. paper) — ISBN 978-0-8143-3808-7 (ebook)
1. Donna Reed show (Television program : 1958–1966) 2. Women on television.
3. Women in popular culture—United States. I. Title.
PN1992.77.D725M67 2012
791.45'72—dc23
2012015782

∞

CONTENTS

ACKNOWLEDGMENTS

I am deeply grateful to all of the people who made this book **vii** possible. I'd like to thank the acquisitions editors, Annie Martin and Kristina Stonehill, who shepherded this book from initial conception to its completion, as well as the series editors Barry Keith Grant and Jeanette Sloniowski and the two anonymous reviewers who made this a stronger book. I'd also like to thank Maya Rhodes for her patience and Yvonne Ramsey for her meticulous copyediting. I'm also appreciative of Mary Owen, who read chapters, helped with photographs, and gave me insight into her wonderful mother.

My friends and colleagues at Northeastern University—Marcus Breen, Murray Forman, Kumi Silva, David Monje, and Craig Robertson—provided me with fortitude, inspiration, and good cheer throughout the writing of this book. They deserve a special thank you. Most of all I'd like to thank my daughter Isabel Lewis, who watched every episode with me and shared her analytic abilities. I couldn't have written this book without her. Emma Lewis also has my gratitude. Her endless energy and exuberance motivate me in all of my endeavors. Richard Lewis inspires me every day. I am ever grateful for his wisdom and generosity.

Finally, I'd like to acknowledge Donna Reed, who quietly created new possibilities for women whether on, behind, or off the screen and who inspired such devotion among those who knew her. Most importantly, I'd like to express my thanks to my own mother, Jennie Morreale. She was a working mother at a time when this was not so common in suburban middle-American households. She created new possibilities for me.

The Donna Reed Show

When most people think of the classic 1950s' television domestic situation comedy, *Father Knows Best* (1954–60), *Leave It to Beaver* (1957–63), and perhaps *The Adventures of Ozzie and Harriet* (1952–66) typically come to mind. Somehow *The Donna Reed Show* rarely comes up first and often doesn't get included at all, even though it had a longer run (1958–66) than either *Leave It to Beaver* or *Father Knows Best*. This isn't because these shows were more popular than *The Donna Reed Show*, as all of these had solid but not outstanding ratings throughout their runs. Familiarity isn't the answer either, as *The Donna Reed Show* aired in twenty-six countries and was syndicated in the United States up until 1994, first on ABC Daytime and then on Nick at Nite and TV Land. Perhaps *The Donna Reed Show* escapes our cultural memory because it does not entirely fit our nostalgic image of the classic 1950s' sitcom.

When *The Donna Reed Show* is mentioned in popular accounts, it is often to posit Donna Reed (rather than her character, Donna Stone) as a complacent supermom. During its run, talk show host David Susskind famously referred to it as "the Madonna Reed Show" (Dern 1963, 11). In *The Erotic Silence of the American Wife*, written in 1992, author Dalma Heyn claims that a woman's personal fulfillment "rests on the murder of Donna Reed" (Fultz 1998, 131). A 2010 poem published in the *Missouri Review* titled "When I Was *The Donna Reed Show*" conveys images of domestic servitude (Seaton 2010, 117). Television shows as disparate as *Cheers, The Nanny,* and *The Gilmore Girls* refer to Donna Reed as the epitome of the perfect mother.[1] Yet what is most striking about popular accounts, beyond the conflation of the character and actress, is that actually watching Donna Reed play Donna Stone reveals that Donna Stone is a complex, even contradictory, character that both is and is not the idealized image of the perfect television mom. Critic Dana Heller's (1995, 47) observation is particularly insightful: "What makes *The Donna Reed Show* a pleasurable narrative spanning generations of viewers is this excess of gender performance, our knowledge of the dark side that threatens to reveal itself, and our trust that in the end Donna will adhere to the script that our collective fantasies of the perfect mother have provided her with." Heller succinctly describes the joys of watching Donna Reed play Donna Stone as she teeters on the edge, constantly threatening to break out of the mold of the 1950s' mom but always incorporated back into the warm embrace of the nuclear family. Perhaps we collectively experience what George Lipsitz (1990, 79–80) refers to as "memory as misappropriation": we remember the past as we wish it had been rather than as it was. Donna Stone is not solely a contented and perfect wife and mother, and the Stones are not the ideal American family. But we don't want to know that.

The Donna Reed Show's protofeminist sensibility may have been due to the fact that Donna Reed was herself a working mother: she was not only the star with four children of her own, but she also had a great deal of creative input into the show. She co-owned and produced the show alongside her husband, Tony Owen. (Screen Gems and Screen Gems executive Irving Briskin were also coproducers.) Todon, the name of the Owen-Reed production company, was an amalgam of both of their first names—a clear homage to Desilu. While Tony Owen handled the financial details, Donna Reed was responsible for the day-to-day production details such as writing, directing, and overseeing sets and costumes. Donna Reed was one of the first female television executives, although her work, like that of so many women in the 1950s, was largely uncredited.[2]

The pilot for *The Donna Reed Show* was sold to ABC for the autumn 1958 season, with Campbell's Soup as its sponsor. Initially the show aired on Wednesday nights at nine o'clock—not a great time for a family comedy even though it followed *The Adventures of Ozzie and Harriet*. The first-season ratings for *The Donna Reed Show* were poor: the Neilsen rating for the first show was 8, with 20 a mark of success for a new show. In those days, however, a sponsor could keep a show on the air, and Campbell's Soup, aligned with a family sitcom for obvious reasons, maintained its support for the show. It may also have helped that *The Donna Reed Show* was up against *The Kraft Music Hall* featuring Milton Berle on NBC at a time when comedy-variety shows were losing popularity. Although *Kraft Music Hall* was cancelled after a few months, *The Donna Reed Show* lasted for eight seasons. In the second season it was moved to eight o'clock on Thursday nights, which was a better time for family viewing. By its third season, it was firmly established in the eight o'clock Thursday evening slot, where it remained throughout its run.

According to some accounts, by 1966 Donna Reed was tired and decided that it was time to stop (although according to Screen Gems executive William Dozier, she routinely—and wisely—made this claim from season 3 on, just prior to her new contract negotiation) ("Wheeling and Dealing" 1962, 20). More likely, *The Donna Reed Show* was a victim of changing times. Ratings had begun falling in the autumn of 1965, and with the industry-wide switch to color television, ABC retired both the long-running *Donna Reed Show* and *The Adventures of Ozzie and Harriet* rather than incur the expenses of making the

3

1964 Cast Photo. (Courtesy of The Donna Reed Foundation)

switch. Their demise marked the end of the classic black-and-white television sitcom that portrayed an idealized suburban nuclear family. The new domestic sitcoms that emerged in the mid-1960s portrayed "strange" families on the margins of suburbia—shows such as *The Addams Family, The Munsters, My Favorite Martian, Bewitched,* and *I Dream of Jeannie.*[3] In the 1970s, beginning with the troika of *M*A*S*H, The Mary Tyler Moore Show,* and *All in the Family,* the sitcom became far more political, and families became far more complicated, even venturing out of the home and into the workplace. Sitcoms such as *The Donna Reed Show* were thought to be representative of a bygone era of television history.

Yet it is time to reclaim *The Donna Reed Show* as a television milestone. The show is an important but overlooked text that provides insight into the interplay of representation, industry, and culture. The series run, from 1958 to 1966, marks a key moment of cultural transition from the conservative 1950s to the more liberal 1960s, and the tensions that accompany this shift are readily observed in the narrative content of the show, particularly with regard to gender and family dynamics. Throughout there is trouble in the text that marks conflicts and contradictions. While none of the 1950s' sitcoms were as conformist and complacent as popular memory would have them, *The Donna Reed Show* was doubly aberrant: in a social and political era known for sitcoms that supported a patriarchal family structure, the show not only starred a woman who headlined her own series but also focused on the mother rather than the father or the children. It was an anomaly to have a woman take the lead, literally and metaphorically, in a family sitcom. Moreover, Donna Reed was an Oscar-winning film actress who crossed over to a television situation comedy as both star and producer. The resultant *Donna Reed Show,* like Donna Reed herself, represented a merger of Hollywood and television and as such provides insight into the relationship between the film and television industries in the late 1950s. It was a Hollywood sitcom that exemplified the synergy that was developing between media industries: *The Donna Reed Show* brought a cinematic aesthetic to the television sitcom, used plot devices to promote the film industry, and manufactured singing careers for its two teenage stars. The show also illustrates the interrelationship of discursive representations from television's past

5

to present. Over the years the show has remained relevant, as indicated by sitcoms that have revisited themes addressed by *The Donna Reed Show*. Overall, *The Donna Reed Show* illuminates the multiple ways that television texts engage in dialogue with their wider cultural contexts.

The Donna Reed Show and Counterreadings of the Sitcom

On the surface, *The Donna Reed Show* is a classic example of the middle-class domestic sitcom that came to dominate television in the 1950s and on into the 1960s. The Stones are a typical nuclear family of the era. They live in the anonymous suburb of Hilldale, somewhere in middle America. Donna Reed plays housewife Donna Stone, while Carl Betz plays her husband, pediatrician Alex Stone. Paul Petersen, who had previously been a Mouseketeer, is twelve-year-old son Jeff, while fourteen-year-old Shelley Fabares, who had been acting since the age of three, is daughter Mary.

Plots are trivial, problems are slight, and many story lines revolve around domestic negotiations or the trials and tribulations of children growing up. The comedy usually involves some mishap that threatens to disrupt familial harmony or the social order, but the problem is always alleviated at the end of the episode. In this particular series, dilemmas are usually resolved by Donna's words or actions. In the series pilot, for example, Donna and Alex's plans for a weekend trip are thwarted when Alex doesn't want to leave a patient who has a mysterious illness. Donna not only finds another doctor to fill in for Alex, but she also determines that the young boy's illness is psychosomatic, a diagnosis that eludes her well-meaning husband. During eight seasons and 275 episodes, there are few plot developments apart from Mary and Jeff's passage from high school to college. There is a narrative reboot in season 5 when the Stones adopt a runaway orphan, Trisha (played by Paul Petersen's sister Patty), after Shelley Fabares left the show. The addition of a new family member is a device frequently used to rejuvenate situation comedies faced with aging children. There is also a slight plot arc in the same season when Alex's friend and colleague Dave Kelsey and his wife Midge move in next door to the Stones. According to Paul Petersen, "ABC thought we needed new neighbors to add a twist to the plot after Shelley left" (Tucker 2007, 114). The Kelseys became part of the show's opening credits in season 6, although they were dropped when Bob Crane, who played Dave Kelsey, left the show the following year to begin work on *Hogan's Heroes*. After Crane left, Ann McCrea, who played Midge, stayed on the show, and Dave Kelsey was simply written out of the story line. Similarly, after Shelley Fabares left the show, Mary's name rarely came up, although her departure was initially explained because Mary moved away to college. There are some recurring neighbors, friends, boyfriends, and girlfriends, but for the most part there are few references to past episodes or unresolved narrative arcs that continue over a number of episodes. There are even inconsistencies in Donna Stone's on-screen biography: she supposedly married at eighteen but somehow had gone to college and worked as a graduate nurse when she met Alex. Accounts of Donna and Alex's courtship also vary, and one episode—"The First Time We Met"—even addresses their conflicting memories. Viewers can tune in and out and follow along effortlessly.

Yet because the situation comedy is a part of the machinery of television involved in making meaning, it is open to multiple interpretations. A recurrent question with regard to sitcoms is whether they are ideologically incorporative, subversive, or capable of both inflections. As noted by Daryl Hamamoto (1989, 27), the situation comedy has always offered oppositional ideas, depicted oppression and struggle, and reflected a critical consciousness that stops just short of political mobilization. For example, Lucy Ricardo, Gracie Allen, and Alice Kramden challenge the domestic constraints imposed on the housewife in early 1950s' television, even though all three rebellious women are consistently put in their places by the narrative's resolution in order to conform to the sitcom's requirement for a return to equilibrium. Even Harriet Nelson, Margaret Anderson, and June Cleaver occasionally chafe at their domestic constraints, though not as consistently as Donna Reed. Paul Wells (1998) writes that subversive discourses often occur within the closed, formulaic, light conventions of the situation comedy, which renders them less threatening while providing a safe site to rehearse the altered roles.

Situation comedies such as *The Donna Reed Show* are thus always open to negotiation, always sites of contestation. While their overt messages may be ideologically incorporative—that is, they may reinforce traditional gender roles, the values of the nuclear family, or the normativity of the medium of television—they may also be open to counterreadings that illuminate their ideological tensions. Lipsitz (1986), in his classic article "The Meaning of Memory: Family, Class and Ethnicity in Early Network Television," has taught us that television programs illuminate societal tensions even though they may resolve them in ideologically complacent ways. He has written extensively about the urban ethnic working-class comedies on television from 1949 to 1957 and specifically cites two early texts—*The Goldbergs* (1949–56) and *Mama* (1949–57)—that served an important function in arbitrating tensions about family identity, consumption, ethnicity, class, and gender roles resulting from economic and social changes in postwar America. A brief foray into the workings of one of these texts—*Mama*—will both contextualize *The Donna Reed Show* and provide insight into the ideological operations of both. *Mama* went off the air just before *The Donna Reed Show* appeared, thus marking the transition from ethnic urban sitcoms to the middle-class domestic sitcom. While *Mama* was more concerned with the conflicts between tradition and modernity, other conflicts, such as those concern-

8

ing gender and the family in the postwar domestic economy, remained central in *The Donna Reed Show*.

Mama was about a Norwegian family, the Hansens, living in San Francisco at the turn of the century. Specifically, Lipsitz (1986, 1990) argues that these programs about ethnic families helped to transform class and ethnic identities into consumer identities by negotiating the cultural transition from an economy of scarcity to one of abundance. This typically played out as a conflict between traditional and modern values. While the resolutions of episodes seemed to reinforce the value of tradition, in the postwar context of modernization and the rise of consumer culture, modern values and commodities were often displayed in the course of the narrative, and the tensions between tradition and modernity often remained unresolved.

For example, in "Mama's Bad Day," youngest daughter Dagmar feigns a stomachache to avoid going to school, daughter Katrin procrastinates about practicing the piano, and husband Jake puts off repairing a set of drawers. When Mama complains to her friend about having to do so much housework, she finds a pack of cigarettes in her son Nils's pocket. She spends all day cooking a meat loaf, only to find that Jake's boss has taken him to lunch at a restaurant and he is not hungry. There is much discussion of eating out at restaurants, which the children see as exemplifying modern life but which Mama sees as a threat. Exasperated with her family, Mama decides to play cards with her friends, an invitation she had declined earlier because her family needed her. Yet as the evening progresses, she becomes overwhelmed by guilt and can't concentrate on her card game. She returns home to find everyone obediently fulfilling their tasks. On the surface it appears that tradition is restored. Yet throughout the narrative viewers have seen Mama's discontent, which is not resolved; have seen the younger generation rebelling against the parents; and have heard about the modern delights of eating in restaurants as opposed to home-cooked meals. Although the emphasis in these shows was on tradition as a source of values, the shows simultaneously promoted new consumer goods and a modern lifestyle, which in fact undermined tradition.

We can always find the ideological fault lines where tensions remain, and *The Donna Reed Show* is a rich site of such tensions. Ethnic identity and traditional values threatened by modernity have been erased in the homogenous middle American suburb of Hilldale, where the Stone family makes its home. Yet tensions around issues such as social status, gender, parenting, and consumer culture mark this new version of the American family. Stated another way, Todd Gitlin (1983, 217) notes that television entertainment takes its design from social and psychological fissures, and success often comes from finding the major value conflicts in society and bridging them. However, conflicts and contradictions are not always resolved. Even a brief survey of television situation comedies demonstrates that while in most cases they attempt to smooth over contradictions, there is often trouble in the text that cannot be contained. This book will focus on the trouble that marks the text of *The Donna Reed Show* as well as its attempts to allay tensions and contradictions.

Social Context of *The Donna Reed Show*

The post–World War II social context of the 1950s and early 1960s elucidates the tensions and contradictions that *The Donna Reed Show* both displayed and mediated. Throughout the 1950s, women were increasingly targeted as consumers and contained within the home. Domestic containment was the corollary to the foreign policy of containment that characterized the postwar stance of the United States. In *Homeward Bound,* Elaine Tyler May (1999) makes the connections between foreign and domestic policies in the postwar period, stating that domestic containment was an outgrowth of the fears and aspirations unleashed after the war. She writes that "Within the home, potentially dangerous social forces of the new age might be tamed, where they could contribute to the secure and fulfilling life to which postwar men and women aspired" (14). On the domestic level, containment was manifest through conformity with the white suburban nuclear family with a heterosexual couple: father who was the breadwinner and mother who was a homemaker. Women in this ideal were feminine but not overtly sexual. Their domain was the kitchen, and their children learned to fit into traditional gender roles. While many married women worked during the Great Depression and were mobilized in the workforce during World War II, after the war television became an important tool for encouraging them to return to the home and to conform to the model of domesticity promoted throughout the culture.

On television, the modern middle-class lifestyle was presented as both desirable and attainable, although it did not include those typically on the bottom of the socioeconomic ladder: immigrants, African Americans, and rural Americans. While the ethnic and working-class sitcoms of television's early period such as *Mama* and *The Goldbergs* addressed class aspirations and the vaudevillian-based showbiz sitcoms such as *Burns and Allen* (1950–58) and *I Love Lucy* (1951–57) offered the lure of modern life, the middle-class domestic sitcoms that followed etched out the lives of the new white culturally assimilated suburban middle class of consumers.

Mary Beth Haralovich (2003, 70), in "Sitcoms and Suburbs: Positioning the 1950s Homemaker," describes how media promotion of an ideal middle-class home life, in concert with government programs, was a primary means of reconstituting and resocializing the American family after World War II. The GI Bill enabled many families to purchase homes and cars because of low-interest loans, although as Haralovich also points out, red-lining practices kept black families out of the suburbs, and the bill's provision for college enrollment largely benefited white men because of college segregation. Women who lost their jobs in the skilled labor force to make room for men returning home from the war were repositioned within the home, which was "sold" to them as a site of leisure and prosperity. Haralovich writes in regard to the suburban homemaker that "She was promised psychic and social satisfaction for being contained within the private space of the home; and in exchange for being targeted, measured, and analyzed for the marketing and design of consumer products, she was promised leisure and freedom from housework" (70).

Thus, the white middle-class family living in the suburbs was the cornerstone of the television sitcom, which positioned the nuclear family as the basic support for consumer culture and the ideology of domestic containment. Television, located within the home, was central to this ideology. The image of the housewife shifted from the portly Gertrude Berg and Marta Hansen to the highly coifed, slim, and attractive figure of Donna Stone. The 1950s' television mothers were sexualized rather than matronly; they were attired in high-heeled shoes and cinch-waist dresses as they bustled about in the kitchen preparing meals for the family. Housework was rarely shown as unpleasant or laborious, as these programs were meant to make the life of the suburban housewife desirable. Donna Stone, however, did physical labor such as vacuuming, repainting the living room, hanging wallpaper, and cleaning out the attic, which provides an indication of how *The Donna Reed Show* was anomalous, given its social context.

The middle-class lifestyle was advertised both within the appliance-laden settings of the programs, through their plots, and in the commercials interspersed between scenes. The families were relatively affluent: homes were laden with possessions, and plots often revolved around acquisition of consumer goods. Programs stressed the values of thrift and responsibility while simultaneously presenting consumption as the core of everyday life. For example, in the "Betty Earns a Formal" episode of *Father Knows Best,* daughter Betty takes a part-time job to pay for an expensive party dress (and much of the plot revolves around her father's consternation that she is working). In the "Ward's Golf Clubs" episode of *Leave It to Beaver,* Beaver believes that he has broken his father's favorite driver and tries to replace it. When Beaver does not have enough money, the store owner gives him (and viewers) instruction and encouragement on installment buying. In the "Charge!" episode of *The Donna Reed Show,* Donna learns that the Stone family does not qualify for a credit card because they do not owe any money. To express her consternation, she takes a pet monkey that Trisha is babysitting to the department store to show that even a monkey can qualify for a credit card. In all cases, the themes stress responsibility while naturalizing consumption.

Moreover, sponsors were involved in every step of a production. In the case of *Donna Reed,* Campbell's Soup and then later Singer Sewing Machines were the most frequent sponsors of the show. Paul Petersen (2008) recalled that "In our day, corporations owned the time and we worked at the end of the day for Campbell's Soup. . . . Our job was to deliver the audience who would go to the supermarket and buy Campbell's Soup." As was a common practice at the time when television stars promoted products, Donna Stone often appeared in commercials both before and during the program, and Donna Reed/Donna Stone was also prominent in print ads for these products at the time. Donna Stone is often seen vacuuming or sewing, and both vacuum cleaners and sewing machines were Singer products. In early episodes when she goes to the grocery store, Campbell's products can be seen on the shelves. *The Donna Reed Show* also introduced Swanson frozen foods, and Jeff always wore Converse sneakers. In at least two episodes the sneakers featured prominently. In "Three Part Mother" when Donna unknots Jeff's shoelaces, the sneakers occupy center frame, with the Converse star clearly exposed. In "The Chinese Horse" when the Stone family fears that there are burglars in the house, Jeff's Converse

13

sneaker becomes his weapon of choice to stave off the imagined intruders.

Out of the seventeen different family sitcoms that aired on network prime-time between 1957 and 1960, fourteen were set in the suburbs, and several domestic sitcoms remained in the Nielsen top 25 until 1964, when their popularity waned (Spigel 1991, 215).[4] These featured the ideal middle-class family consisting of a father who was the decision maker, busy with his work but present for his wife and children; a mother who sublimated her needs to her family; and children who were spunky but ultimately well behaved. Story lines stressed values such as hard work, honesty, responsibility, and the importance of the nuclear family, and the lessons learned often taught these values. While the ethnic and working-class sitcoms of television's early period dealt with the conflicts between tradition and modernity, the middle-class domestic sitcoms such as *The Donna Reed Show* etched out an idealized vision of the lives of the new suburban class of consumers.

In this context, the now classic domestic sitcoms such as *The Adventures of Ozzie and Harriet, Father Knows Best, Leave It to Beaver,* and *The Donna Reed Show* presented a nuclear family surrounded by the stuff of middle-class life in a world defined by consensus. Yet the cultural transition to postwar life, while depicted on television in terms of domestic harmony and economic prosperity, was also wrought with tensions and contradictions. The real-life Korean War, Cold War, racial and class divisions, bored and stifled housewives, and decaying inner cities were not part of the television landscape. Under scrutiny, the classic domestic sitcoms show cracks in the edifice of the harmonious family. In describing their underside, John Ellis (2000, 119) states that "They showed the struggle with new kinds of domestic space and machinery (not least the television itself); the negotiation with new neighbors; the isolation of women and the frustration of their desires for an identity in the world; the separation of couples through commuting;

even the emergence of bored youth and the teenager as a social category." With the exception of commuting (Alex Stone first had an office in the house and then moved to another space in Hilldale), these issues identify the trouble in the text of *The Donna Reed Show.*

By the early 1960s, critiques of suburbia and domestic containment were emerging in popular media. Betty Friedan's *The Feminine Mystique,* published in 1963, received widespread support for its attack on sexism and patriarchal ideology and is largely credited with shaping the subsequent second-wave women's movement. *The Donna Reed Show* subtly negotiates the transition from the conservative 1950s to the liberal 1960s, particularly apparent in episodes in which Donna asserts her independence or Mary and Jeff navigate teen culture. For example, although the opening credits of *The Donna Reed Show* remain structurally similar throughout its eight seasons, by 1966 they indicate that Donna Stone has a public life outside of the home. In season 1, the "Happy Days" theme music is slow, the graphics are solid and classic, and all the characters, including Donna, are framed by a medium shot as Donna answers the phone and then sees each family member off as they leave for the day. By season 2, the music speeds up, the lettering is asymmetrical, and the camera lingers on Donna, who gets a medium close-up when she answers the phone. By season 8, the music is jazzy. Donna's hair is lighter and in a fashionable bob. She wears a suit, a thick string of pearls adorns her neck, and she carries a purse. She still kisses Alex and the children goodbye as they leave for the day (although here it is Jeff and Trisha rather than Jeff and Mary). But in all of the previous seasons, Donna places her hand on her hip and smiles contentedly after she shuts the door, as if her job in getting the family out into the world was complete. In season 8, though, she glances at her watch, gasps, grabs her purse, and rushes off to her own appointment.

Middle-class men too were increasingly aware of the limitations of middle-class prosperity. Influential books such as David Riesman's *The Lonely Crowd* (1950) and William Whyte's *The Organization Man* (1956) critiqued the way that postwar culture produced a middle class defined by conformity and consensus. Many of the jobs for middle-class men were in large impersonal corporations located in cities where they commuted to work, and they served as the sole economic support for their families by becoming anonymous organization men enmeshed in bureaucratic structures. Historians and critics have written about how the values of teamwork, cooperation, and conformity required in the shift from a production-based economy to a consumption-based economy threatened male authority and produced a crisis of masculinity in the 1950s.[5] These tensions contributed to a widespread sense of disillusionment that did not coincide with the images of the idealized nuclear family in domestic sitcoms.

16

The period roughly from 1958 to 1966, the run of *The Donna Reed Show,* marked the standardization of the domestic sitcom genre while also indicating subtle shifts and undercurrents of unrest within the culture. This book illustrates the way that *The Donna Reed Show* articulates cultural tensions while continuing to naturalize the white middle-class nuclear family. I divide it into five chapters. Chapter 1 locates Donna Reed in relation to her predecessors Gertrude Berg and Lucille Ball, who were strong female presences both in front of and behind the camera. I argue that Donna Reed was similarly influential and that the show addressed progressive themes, although she downplayed her influence and stayed behind the scenes. Chapter 2 focuses on the telefilm aesthetics of *The Donna Reed Show.* I argue that *The Donna Reed Show* is a prime example of the emergent synergy between Hollywood and the television industry in the late 1950s. Many of the writers and directors came to the show after working in Hollywood, and many of the resultant episodes exhibit a cinematic aesthetic that enters into dialogue with sitcom form and content. Next, in chapter 3 I discuss Donna Reed in relation to feminism by considering her femininity as a masquerade. While there have been feminist readings of women in early sitcoms, little work has been done on *The Donna Reed Show*. It is commonly argued that 1950s' sitcoms, in a postwar period in which women were being encouraged to return to the home in order to make space for men in the workplace, both marginalized the figure of the housewife and attempted to domesticate women by promoting a suburban life of leisure based around consumption. While *The Donna Reed Show* exemplifies the domestic containment of women in the postwar period and while Donna Stone wears the mask of femininity, there are several episodes in which she performs a different identity and contests her prescribed role in the private and public sphere. In chapter 4 I consider the show's representation of teen culture. Both Mary and Jeff Stone attend high school and then college during the course of the show's run. At a time when the teen counterculture was developing, Donna Stone's parenting style addressed discourses around permissive parenting that were prevalent in the culture. Yet for the most part the show ignored generational conflict. The show participated in popular culture primarily by launching the singing careers of its two young stars, although a few episodes addressed social tensions around teen rebellion and the counterculture. Finally, in chapter 5 I consider the legacy of *The Donna Reed Show*. Just as the Donna Stone character provided a protofeminist model for housewives, *The Donna Reed Show* was a harbinger of the progressive values that appear in later sitcoms, and its dialogue with contemporary television texts speaks to its enduring place in television history.

Women behind the Screens

Donna Reed Backstage

Although the character of Donna Stone is far removed from the life of film star Donna Reed, *The Donna Reed Show* deliberately conflates the two. Donna Stone's maiden name is Mullenger, and she comes from Iowa. Similarly, Donna Reed was born Donna Mullenger in Denison, Iowa, on January 27, 1921. The oldest of five siblings, she grew up on a farm in Iowa during the Great Depression, and her midwestern good sense is often attributed to the character of Donna Stone. "It may have been good training for life, but we had few good times and very little money," Donna Reed said of her upbringing (Tucker 2007, 109). After high school, she moved to Los Angeles to live with an aunt and enrolled in Los Angeles City College, where she sought a secretarial degree but took courses in theater and drama. While still in college, Reed won a beauty contest in 1940 and got her picture on the front page of the *Los Angeles Times,* which caught the attention of movie studios. MGM gave her a screen test and put her under contract, changing her name from Donna Mullenger to Donna Reed. She immediately got roles in several MGM B films of such ilk as *The Getaway* and *Shadow of the Thin*

Man in 1941 and *The Courtship of Andy Hardy* in 1942. At this time she met makeup artist William Tuttle, whom she married in 1943 and divorced in 1945. Her biography, written by Fultz (1998), portrays her as ambitious and career-driven, always seeking a breakthrough role that would move her to the A list.

Throughout her Hollywood career, Donna Reed was typecast as the good girl, a role she later reprised in *The Donna Reed Show*. She received two memorable film roles in 1945 while still under contract to MGM: she played the niece of the artist who painted *The Picture of Dorian Gray* and was the nurse in John Ford's *They Were Expendable*. She wanted the racier part of the tavern singer in *Dorian Gray* but was relegated to the secondary role. This was also the year she married Tony Owen, who was her agent. She went on to star in *It's a Wonderful Life* a year later, although its lukewarm box office reception at the time did little to help her career. Overall she was unhappy with her film roles, as she was primarily cast in supporting roles or B movies, and when her contract with MGM expired, she left to freelance and raise her children: a daughter adopted in 1946, a son adopted in 1947, and a natural son born in 1949.

Tony Owen worked as assistant to Columbia Pictures head Harry Cohn. Perhaps not coincidentally, Reed secured a contract there in 1950, and later the Columbia Pictures' television arm, Screen Gems, became coproducer of *The Donna Reed Show*. When Owen decided to pursue a career as a film producer, Reed became the major financial support for the family. In 1953 she secured the role that won her an Oscar for Best Supporting Actress, playing a prostitute in the World War II drama *From Here to Eternity*. Yet even after she won the Oscar she continued to be typecast, and Columbia followed up with more roles in B movies. She left Columbia and signed with Universal but ended up suing for breach of contract when the company only offered her supporting roles instead of the starring roles that she had been promised.

In 1958 Donna Reed left films for television, citing lack of good film roles for women and financial security as her reasons. She was also thirty-seven years old, which meant that she was past her prime in Hollywood, and by that time she had four children, which made traveling for long film shoots difficult. (She gave birth to a daughter, Mary, in 1957.) According to Fultz (1998), Reed and Owen saw an opportunity in television; the television industry was in the midst of making the shift from New York to Hollywood, and by 1957 television was already in forty million homes. At the time, the two most popular television genres were sitcoms and westerns, and since westerns rarely had women in lead roles, Owen and Reed decided on a sitcom. At first they thought of making her a single secretary and then a diplomat's wife, which were two familiar tropes at the time. The idea to cast Donna Reed as a version of herself came from a Columbia executive who saw a photograph of Reed surrounded by her children and younger sister and suggested that she play herself—a wife and mother (Fultz 1998, 117). They decided on casting Reed as Donna Stone, a middle-class housewife who lived in Hilldale, an unspecified midwestern town (although it always seemed to be summer).

MGM screenwriter William Roberts, a Hollywood veteran whose credits included *The Magnificent Seven,* created the characters and wrote several episodes of the show. He intended for it to be about the many conflicting demands on the stay-at-home mom, who was expected to be "wife, mother, companion, booster, nurse, housekeeper, cook, laundress, gardener, bookkeeper, clubwoman, choir singer, PTA officer, Scout leader, and at the same time, effervescent, immaculate, and pretty" (Tucker 2007, 114). The choice of a pediatrician who was often on call was deliberate, because according to Fultz (1998, 118), "it allowed Donna the domestic forefront without sacrificing the authority of Dr. Alex Stone, whose office was in a back room at home." His busy job frequently took him out of the home and provided the pretext for the primacy of the mother.

The writers were told to make her "a strong character that reacted to situations dynamically, and her views did not need to always coincide with her husband's" (Grimes 1960). While Roberts oversaw most of the episodes, there were several directors and writers throughout the series. Established film directors such as Oscar Rudolph, Andrew McCullough, Norman Tokar, and Ida Lupino (one of the few female directors in Hollywood) brought their skills to the show, as did several writers who became known for their work in television in later years: Nate Monaster, John Whedon, Phil Sharp, and Barbara Avedon. The result was a family comedy that combined the sentimentality of melodrama with humorous everyday situations, and its sensibility was, according to Reed, progressive. "We started breaking rules left and right" she said. "We had a female lead, for one thing, a strong, healthy woman. We had a story line told from a woman's point of view that wasn't soap opera" (Tucker 2007, 114). Donna Reed was nominated for an Emmy four times for her work on the show, and although she never won, she received a Golden Globe for Best Actress in a Television Series in 1963.

Because of their debt to commercial sponsorship, most sitcoms, then as now, were reluctant or unable to take controversial positions on social issues. While *The Donna Reed Show* was not overtly political, throughout the series' run some of its writers tried to "smuggle in" socially progressive images and themes. Consistent with late 1950s' sitcoms, there were few ethnic characters, and many of those that did appear on the show—such as the Italian milkman or Irish housekeeper—were portrayed as Other, either lower class or not culturally assimilated. In 1959, writer Nate Monaster managed to have a black woman and her daughter included in the background of a scene in a department store, but even as late as 1965 he could not write black characters into story lines. When he wrote a part for a black boy as one of the Stones' neighbors, the network and sponsors demanded that the boy become white so that the show would not be kept off the air in the South (Fultz 1998, 129). In the final season, however, a black secretary was cast in the episode "Trees," and there were black teenagers dancing to rock and roll in "Pop Goes Theresa," although no black characters ever appeared in recurring roles.

Barbara Avedon wrote many episodes with a feminist slant. Avedon is best known as the writer and cocreator of *Cagney and Lacey* (1981–88), which was the first television drama to star two strong independent women. Her sensibilities were apparent in *The Donna Reed Show*. For example, in "Rebel with a Cause," Donna becomes resentful after participating in a marketing survey of housewives; in "Pioneer Woman," Donna attempts to prove that women are as capable as men; and in "Author, Author," Donna decides to take up a writing career. While always a strong character, Donna Stone chafes against gender inequality in episodes penned by Avedon.

There were also writers who had been blacklisted during the infamous communist scare of the 1950s. Alfred Lewis Levitt wrote under the name Tom August and was joined by his wife Helen, who also wrote under the name August. During the first season, Tom August wrote the episode "It's The Principle of the Thing" that critiqued consumerism through the eyes of a proud Italian immigrant. Both Tom and Helen August wrote the episode "Geisha Girl" in 1961. Singer and actress Myoshi Umeki, the first Asian to win an Oscar, guest starred as a Japanese woman whose husband brings her to live in Hilldale. The twist is not that the women of Hilldale have trouble accepting the ethnic Other but rather that they are appalled that she gives her husband a nightly massage, serves him dinner, and lights his cigar and that he lets her carry the groceries as she walks four paces behind him. They become affronted that she waits on him while he does nothing to help. In the end, she explains that she chooses to behave this way because it is her custom. But Donna decides to teach her the American way of life, which is learned by purchasing products. The two go on a shopping

23

spree, and the traditional geisha girl emerges with new clothing and a modern hairstyle. In the end, she resolves to change her ways to adapt to her new culture. While the message is one that reinforces the "rightness" of assimilated consumerist middle-class American behavior, there is also an impulse toward equality (although the affronted women do not see that they too wait on their husbands and are subservient, if in a less obvious manner). The episode ends on an ironic note, with the Japanese woman effortlessly giving her husband a massage with an electric tool and a cut to Donna grudgingly massaging Alex's back with her hands.

The Donna Reed Show was also one of the first television sitcoms to showcase professional athletes, beginning in a first-season episode, "All Mothers Worry," in which several members

"Geisha Girl" guest starred singer and Oscar-winning actress Myoshi Umeki. (Courtesy of The Donna Reed Foundation)

of the Los Angeles Rams appeared as themselves. In 1960 as physical fitness became an early focus of the John F. Kennedy presidency, Alfred Lewis Levitt and Helen Levitt penned "The Perfect Pitch," in which Don Drysdale appeared in a cameo role. Both Drysdale and Willie Mays appeared together in "My Son the Catcher in 1966," and Mays also played himself in "Calling Willie Mays" in 1966.

Sitcom Women behind the Scenes

From Donna Reed's earliest days under contract to MGM, her film roles and the offscreen persona that the studio encouraged her to cultivate portrayed her as a wholesome "good girl." According to Philip French (2010, 14), "Every studio had its 'girl-next-door' under contract in the 30s and 40s: a pretty, whole-some, reliable future homemaker, usually a small town girl from the Midwest." According to Donna Reed's first husband Bill Tuttle, the studio governed every aspect of her personal life, even chastising her once for getting an ice cream cone while dressed in casual clothes. During World War II she was one of many starlets who toured army bases, while MGM continued to emphasize her wholesome image. She personally answered many letters and kept many of those that were written to her (which were recently released by her daughter Mary Owen). In 1944, aided by the MGM publicity department, a U.S. battalion stationed in Europe voted her "The girl I'd most like to come home to."

However, Donna Reed was more complicated than her syrupy image implied. She also posed topless for a glamour magazine early in her career, aborted an inconvenient pregnancy when married to Bill Tuttle, and tried to break free of the limited roles that typecast her. She fought to get the role of the prostitute Alma in *From Here to Eternity* and only succeeded because of the influence of Columbia mogul Harry Cohn. In later years she complained that she had not been offered challenging roles, despite winning an Oscar for her work in *From Here to Eternity*. She was also cynical about Hollywood and the male producers in control. Most famously, she noted, "Forty pictures I was in, and all I remember is, 'What kind of bra will you be wearing today, honey?' That was always the area of big decision—from the neck to the navel" (Donna Reed Quotes n.d.).

When Donna Reed moved to television, she parlayed her image as the wholesome girl next door to the woman this girl became when she got married—the perfect wife and homemaker. While the show clearly traded on her star appeal, throughout its run publicity emphasized her ordinariness and reproduced her wholesome image. This domestication of the female star allayed the threat posed by a powerful woman who produced her own television show. Photographs of Donna's real children were paired with her television family, erasing the distinction between Donna Reed and Donna Stone. In an ad for Campbell's Soup, Donna Reed advises women to save labels from cans to trade in for mugs or bowls as theme music from *The Donna Reed Show* plays in the background. Interviews continually stressed her midwestern farm girl roots and the fact that she was herself a mother in order to appeal to viewers in the more intimate context of television. For example, in a 1958 *TV Guide* article titled "Just What the Doctor Ordered" (1958, 11), Carl Betz is quoted as saying that "Donna misses her children. Some days it's obvious that she's depressed, although she'll deny it. Then Tony will call home and have the nurse bring the baby to the set, and sometimes all the kids if it's after school. Then she's happy for the rest of the day." Later the same *TV Guide* article describes her Iowan roots: "She can still bake bread and once won $50 from Lionel Barrymore on a bet that she could milk a cow" (11). Despite the fact that Fultz (1998) reported that her marriage was strained and marked by Tony Owen's philandering (she divorced Owen soon after the show ended), she gave advice on relationships in magazine articles such as "It's Worth Fighting to Save a Marriage," in which she discussed the difficulties and rewards—mostly rewards—of marriage: "We all have those 'down' moments in a marriage when we think the whole thing is falling apart. But you know, how many of us wives who complain could live without marriage now? My husband and my family mean everything to me—they're my world—and it's a wonderful feeling to know we're all growing together" (Christy 1960, 71).

Magazines also printed recipes such as "Bundt Cake a la Donna Reed," further merging the actress with the character. Through her fictional television program, the real Donna Reed became the iconic image of the American mom. In 1959 she received a special citation from the American Mother's Committee, founders of Mother's Day, for her portrayal of Donna Stone.

Reed did, however, express disdain for the situation comedy. While in many ways her show fits neatly into the 1950s' domestic sitcom genre, it departs from conventional representations. For example, in 1963 she was quoted in *TV Radio Mirror* as saying that "I don't portray the All-American Mom, and Carl Betz is not the All-American Daddy, either. So help me, if we had to do *that* type of TV mother and father every week, I'd go off my rocker. Our stories do not revolve only around the kids" (Field 1963). Many episodes focus on Donna and Alex, and it is not uncommon for one or both to express their frustration with the children. Todon Productions insisted on letting Reed lose her temper on the show. In a 1959 *TV Guide* article, Reed discusses the show's climb in the ratings despite the fact that no changes were made: "The only thing I can say is that we were a little late in persuading the sponsor to let us lose our tempers on the show. I mean, the sponsor didn't want Donna Stone, my character, to ever be mean. Tony and I have a family of our own, and there is no such thing as a family where arguments don't occur. Keep it goody-goody and you lose the effectiveness" ("Never Argue with a Woman" 1959, 11).

In accordance with 1950s' ideology, however, Reed stayed behind the scenes, although she was an uncredited producer

27

and director who studied and mastered lighting and cinematography, roles rarely handled by women at that time (Donna Reed Foundation for the Performing Arts n.d.). According to Shelley Fabares, Reed meticulously oversaw every detail of the show's production. She made casting decisions and came up with story ideas. Fabares stated in an interview that "Today on a credit we'd list her as coproducer. Everybody always put Lucy as the only woman who ever did that. That of course is not true. Donna in her quiet way was very much a producer and a writer and a real force behind the show. She was that show" (Fabares 1998). Writers called Reed "the steel fist in the velvet glove," and Andrew McCullough noted that "At conferences she picked up what was wrong with a script and how to fix it, and at first the writers didn't like it. So she had to play the part of a woman—she had to shift from saying, 'You know, we need a scene outside the house where this can happen,' to saying 'Well I don't know anything about writing, but just as a woman it would be difficult to do this.' Then the writers would gladly fix it" (Fultz 1998, 131). Similarly, Screen Gems executive William Dozier remarked that while "Donna is one of the brightest gals in Hollywood, you couldn't have her that way on the show. No one would watch" (Dern 1963, 12).

Predecessors: Gertrude Berg and Lucille Ball

Like Gertrude Berg of *The Goldbergs* and Lucille Ball of *I Love Lucy*, Donna Reed was one of the few women in television to produce and star in her own series, even if she needed to resort to Donna Stone–like manipulations in order to exert her control.[1] In this way, she followed the domestic comedy path first forged by Berg. Berg was one of the unheralded pioneers of early television who was writer, producer, performer, and CEO of *The Goldbergs,* which aired on radio from 1929 to 1949 and then made the transition to television from 1949 to 1955 (Smith 2007, 9). In an industry dominated by males, Berg was completely in charge of *The Goldbergs*. She handled all aspects of the show's production, wrote every episode of the show, and has been credited as "the founder of the family situation comedy on television and radio" (Timberg n.d.).

Berg, like Reed, played a version of herself, drawing on her own background as a Jewish immigrant. As with Reed, the boundaries that marked Berg's public persona and the character she played on television were often intentionally blurred. Even in the 1930s, Berg had an advice column called "Mama Talks" that ran in newspapers, and "Berg's Jewish Cookbook" is still in press today. She played a working-class Jewish housewife, Molly Goldberg, who lived in the Bronx with her extended family. The warm and matronly Molly Goldberg was the family matriarch, and stories revolved around her, much as Donna Stone was often the axial character in *The Donna Reed Show*. Berg's character was quite typical of comic female representations that last until this day: a kind but somewhat scatterbrained housewife whose good intentions lead to comic mishaps. Berg insisted that no laugh track be used, which may account for why *The Goldbergs* is not always included in discussions of the sitcom genre or histories of television comedy. As in later sitcoms such as *The Donna Reed Show*, humor was based on characters and relationships rather than on physical comedy. The verbal humor, largely based on Molly's skewering of language, drew on the vaudeville tradition of ethnic dialogue, although Berg was a refined Columbia graduate with no Yiddish accent. In contrast, in *The Donna Reed Show*, part of the next generation of comedy that contended with the postwar ideology of domestic containment, the Donna Stone character was genteel, fashionable, and devoid of ethnicity, and her character was less the cause of mishaps than the means to their resolution. Yet Reed, like Berg, had a strong point of view that she expressed in her show.

Although *The Goldbergs* was popular in its first two years, it lost its sponsor, Sanka Coffee, in 1951 when Philip Loeb, who played Gertrude's husband Jake, was blacklisted. General Foods demanded that Berg fire Loeb. The show went on hiatus as Berg defended Loeb and argued for keeping him on the show. According to her biographer Glenn D. Smith (2007, 122), "She challenged the corporate sponsors with the threat of withdrawing her own power as the embodiment of consumer culture. One word from the authorizing presence of 'Molly Goldberg' and Sanka sales rose by 57%." But Berg eventually capitulated, and *The Goldbergs* reappeared on NBC in 1952 with a new actor playing Molly's husband and a new sponsor. (Loeb committed suicide in 1955.) While Berg, under direct pressure, attempted to exert her power in the industry, Reed had a quieter but equally influential presence. With regard to blacklisted writers Alfred Lewis Levitt and Helen Slote Levitt, who wrote for the show as Tom and Helen August, Fultz (1998, 130) writes that "The Levitts always felt that Donna knew their true identity and let them keep on working."

The Goldbergs did not fare well after its hiatus, as a new generation of domestic comedies—such as *I Love Lucy, Our Miss Brooks* (1952–56), *I Married Joan* (1952–55), and *The Adventures of Ozzie and Harriet*—were appealing to viewers and corporate sponsors by portraying a middle-class suburban lifestyle and a less ethnic style of humor. The female leads became less matronly and more sexually attractive as they promoted the middle-class life of leisure—enter Lucy Ricardo and Gracie Allen, followed by Margaret Anderson, June Cleaver, and then Donna Stone. Berg attempted to accommodate this shift to the modern domestic sitcom in the final seasons of the show. *The Goldbergs* became *Molly* in 1955, and the family was completely assimilated into the middle class as they moved out of the Bronx and into the suburb of Haverville. (*Molly* aired in syndication only.) In Haverville, the Goldbergs lived in a comfortably appointed detached house, the children attended college, and Jake Goldberg owned his own business. None of their neighbors were Jewish, and Molly's accent became far less pronounced as they merged into the melting pot.

Like *The Donna Reed Show*, *The Goldbergs* addressed tensions around gender equality that were always resolved at the episode's end, although the issues they raised remained salient. In "Molly's Dream" (a 1955 episode of *Molly* rather than *The Goldbergs*), Molly is invited to join the Parents and Teachers Committee in Haverville. As she hangs the laundry to dry, she tells Uncle David, "With my washing and my ironing and my cooking and my cleaning, who has time for such things? After all, I'm not a social butterfly. I'm a housewife. I'll have to recline [*sic*] the invitation." When she sees her neighbor Ms. Van Ness, an amateur psychologist, Molly relates a dream she had where the world was a revolving globe, and she was walking on top of it with a broom, a dust rag, and a mop. "The faster it was revolving, the faster I was wiping," she explains. Ms. Van Ness interprets her dream to mean that Molly is frustrated because she wants to be a part of the world but is "imprisoned" as a housefrau. Molly initially protests that she loves cooking, cleaning, and washing but then concludes that her dreams are telling her that she should become more involved in the world outside of the home. She begins attending meetings, even staying out until one o'clock in the morning. Oddly, no one in the family seems to mind, and Uncle David cheerfully assumes her domestic chores, donning an apron as he hangs the laundry and cooks and serves dinner. Molly keeps recounting her dreams to her neighbor, who continues to interpret them to mean that Molly is frustrated and suppressed. Finally, Molly dreams that her vacuum cleaner has sucked up her husband Jake and the children. They scream "Let me out!" but she locks the vacuum in the closet instead. Mrs. Van Ness tells her that the dream means that she hates her husband and that she feels that her children are obstacles and has a death wish toward them.

In "Molly's Dream," we see Molly moving tentatively toward public life in a way that is quite natural to Donna Stone, who

31

is involved with any number of boards and committees. The idea that Molly may be fulfilled by community involvement or by expressing herself through music (the subject of another dream) is broached but then ultimately dismissed at the end of the episode. Molly becomes upset by the interpretation of her final dream, which seems to be corroborated when she accidentally pulls Rosalie's hair and then makes Jake goulash for dinner, and both independently ask her if she is trying to kill them. Finally, to allay Molly's fear, Uncle David advises Jake to invent a dream that the neighbor will interpret incorrectly. The ploy works. Molly has sudden awareness that her friend is not an authority on dreams, and what is really important is that the family loves one another and should stay together. Despite the fact that the interpretations seemed quite logical, even for an amateur, in the end Molly is content to remain in the house.

Molly was not a success, and when it went off the air in 1956 there were no other completely female-centric domestic comedies left on television. There was one other attempt to produce a sitcom that headlined a woman prior to *The Donna Reed Show*. Stage and film actress Eve Arden had achieved success with the sitcom *Our Miss Brooks,* which began in 1952 and was canceled in 1956. *The Eve Arden Show,* a sitcom about a widowed working mother of two daughters, attempted to bank on her popularity but lasted only a few episodes, and Arden had no behind-the-scenes control. The conflict between home and career that formed the premise of the show may not have fit with the cultural ethos of the 1950s, when women were being urged to remain within the home. The more successful *I Love Lucy,* which ran from 1951 to 1957, dealt with the same themes, although it was in the context of a more traditional domestic arrangement. Lucy Ricardo was a rebellious housewife who wanted to break into show business, while her husband Ricky wanted her to stay at home. Moreover, the theme was overlaid with viewers' knowledge of the real-life marriage of stars Lucille Ball and Desi Arnaz. According to Patricia Mellencamp (1986,

88), "In the elemental, repetitive narrative, Lucy never got what she wanted: a job and recognition. Weekly, for six years, she accepted domesticity, only to try to escape again the next week. During each program, however, she not only succeeded, but demolished Ricky's act . . . and got exactly what she and the television audience wanted: Lucy the star, performing off-key, crazy, perfectly executed vaudeville turns—physical comedy as few women (particularly beautiful ones, former Goldwyn girls) have ever done."

Lucille Ball is the television actress whose career most closely parallels that of Donna Reed, in terms of the conflating of the image of star and performer and in terms of their roles as powerful women both in front of the camera and behind the scenes. Before demure suburban housewives dominated the television landscape, Lucille Ball's Lucy Ricardo was a strong female presence, one of the few women on television to successfully perform physical comedy. The Desilu business model and professional relationship between husband and wife no doubt exerted a strong influence on Donna Reed and her husband Tony Owen, whose Todon Productions borrows the Desilu concept of forming a company name out of the combination of husband's and wife's names, with the husband's name first.

Lucille Ball, like Donna Reed, had been a film actress but had never broken out of B movies, and few of her films were memorable. She was best known for her radio comedy *My Favorite Husband,* which provided the impetus for CBS to ask her for a television adaptation. In the early days of television, many popular sitcoms came from radio (such as *The Goldbergs*). Because of the competition between film and television, there were few film stars willing to work on television. Lucille Ball was a film actress with a bankable name who was willing to do television, so she had some influence with CBS executives. She demanded that the show costar her husband, bandleader Desi Arnaz, so that they could spend more time together rather than endure the constant separations that two careers demanded.

33

CBS balked at the idea. In the conservative 1950s, they were not sure that audiences would accept an "interracial" marriage between a Cuban and a Scotch-Irish American. In order to prove to sponsors that the show was viable, Ball and Arnaz formed their own production company, Desilu, and produced a vaudeville act that they took on the road. When audiences responded favorably and CBS agreed to produce the show, Ball and Arnaz agreed to take reduced salaries in exchange for part ownership of the company. Unlike Todon Productions, which dissolved after the demise of *The Donna Reed Show*, Desilu went on to become a major force in the industry as it took on additional television projects and expanded its base.

CBS wanted to call the series *The Lucille Ball Show*, although Ball insisted that Arnaz share star billing. The compromise became *I Love Lucy*, with the "I" putting Desi Arnaz first. Sponsor Philip Morris demanded, however, that the show was to be a comedy rather than a variety or music program that would serve Arnaz's talents. At a time when many comedies still featured singing and dancing interludes that were not connected to the narrative, Arnaz's contract stipulated that he was to perform musical numbers only when they were integral to the plot (Tucker 2007, 44). Producer Jesse Oppenheimer decided that the Ricardos needed neighbors to liven up the plots, a device that was also adopted successfully by *The Donna Reed Show*, although the Kelseys never received the acclaim awarded Fred and Ethel Mertz, played by William Frawley and Vivian Vance.

While both Lucille Ball and Donna Reed were active owners and participants in their respective production companies, both credited their husbands as producers. Ball eventually became sole owner of Desilu when she bought Arnaz out after their divorce in 1962, which made her the first woman to head a major studio and one of the most powerful women in Hollywood, but in the days of *I Love Lucy*, she remained an unheralded presence. Similar to the character Lucy Ricardo, Ball liked to work, and after *I Love Lucy* ended in 1957 (due to her divorce from

Arnaz), she went on to star in *The Lucy Show*. Donna Reed, on the other hand, was less enamored of headlining another television program. In fact, she once stated that being on a sitcom was "about as glamorous as working on a chain gang" (Fultz 1998, 126).

In contrast to Donna Reed, Lucille Ball was a comedian more so than an actress, and the genius of *I Love Lucy* was to showcase her physical slapstick comedy so that the show existed in the interstices of vaudeville and the domestic sitcom. According to Mellencamp (1986, 87), she "constantly attempted to escape domesticity—her 'situation,' her job in the home—always trying to get into show business by getting into Ricky's act, narratively fouling it up, but brilliantly and comically performing in it." Part of the pleasure for audiences was the show's conflation of Lucille Ball and Lucille Ricardo, and the audience saw, week after week, a woman performing the comic role that the narrative forbid her. Yet if considered on the narrative level alone, *I Love Lucy* is as ideologically conservative as *The Donna Reed Show*, which seemingly portrays the housewife as devoted to the maintenance of family structure rather than trying to escape it. Doyle Greene (2008, 43) writes on this note that "By depicting Lucy Ricardo as an object of audience scorn, someone whose desperate attempts to transcend the barriers of her living conditions are both mockingly amusing and shamelessly wretched, the 'hidden message' that the 'woman's place was in the home' was none-too-hidden at all: *any* attempt by Lucy to transcend her domestic role was not only unsuccessful, but a dismal disaster of slapstick comedy."

Overall, *The Donna Reed Show* owed far more to the melodrama of *The Goldbergs* than the physical comedy of *I Love Lucy*, particularly as Donna Reed never considered herself a comedian and was worried in the early days of the show that she could not play comedy. Donna Stone did not typically "perform" her comedy, although there were a few episodes that were exceptions. For example, one season 2 episode of *The Donna Reed*

Show nods to Lucille Ball–style physical comedy, although it is in the context of an accident rather than the character's rebelliousness. In "Sleep No More My Lady," Donna travels to a convention in New York with Alex, who is delivering a paper. She is overexcited and can't sleep on the plane. Alex offers to give her a sedative, but she declines. He secretly puts two sleeping pills into a cup of warm milk. Unaware of his action, when Alex falls asleep Donna decides to take a few pills after all. When they arrive in New York, she stumbles into the hotel room and collapses on the bed. They learn that Alex must deliver his paper immediately, and Donna, despite being groggy, insists on attending. Alex is at the podium when Donna emerges onto the stage behind him. She wends her way to a chair but cannot stay awake. She yawns loudly and first drops her head on the woman to her left and then leans on the shoulder of the prestigious Dr. Spaulding to her right. In a rather unusual shot, there is a close-up of her dangling foot as her shoe falls onto the floor. When Alex sharply rebukes her with "Donna!" she jumps up and then slumps in her chair and falls to the ground. Alex's presentation is cut short, and they are the laughing stock of the conference. On *I Love Lucy* such behavior would have exasperated Ricky, and Lucy's plight would have been the result of her own machinations. Here Donna Stone is blameless, and Alex staunchly supports her when she is embarrassed after she realizes what she has done. And unlike in *I Love Lucy*, which usually ends with Ricky forgiving Lucy for her transgressions, here Donna Stone herself saves the day by winning over Dr. Spaulding, who allows Alex to finish delivering his paper the next day.

Gertrude Berg and Lucille Ball provided models of successful women who both starred in their own sitcoms and owned their own production companies. Gertrude Berg, from an earlier television generation, was the most powerful woman behind the scenes, although her character Molly Goldberg was hardly an independent feminist icon. Ball indicates the beginnings of the ideological shift from the late 1940s to the 1950s. She is attractive rather than matronly, lives in an urban rather than suburban environment, and is married to a Cuban who owns a nightclub. She is also frustrated rather than contented by her enforced domesticity. Yet both on and off the screen Lucy deferred to her husband, and it was not until she took sole ownership of Desilu in 1962 that she became as powerful as Berg. After Berg and Ball, women who were both actresses and producers largely disappeared from television, with the exception of Reed. Reed, a product of 1950s' ideology that required women to be seen and not heard, exerted her control quietly but effectively. Donna Reed, like Donna Stone, always got her way.

The Donna Reed Show
and the Hollywood Sitcom

*T*he Donna Reed Show* emerged at a key transitional moment of the television industry in terms of both the development of the sitcom genre and the shift from New York to Hollywood as the locus of television production. The emergence of the domestic sitcom that featured white middle-class suburban families, while tied to postwar social changes, is related to the shift from radio to television in the late 1940s as well as the emerging synergy between Hollywood and the television industry in the 1950s. *The Donna Reed Show,* whose star, producers, and often writers and directors came from Hollywood, exemplifies this crossover between the live radio-influenced television sitcom genre and the production techniques and aesthetics of Hollywood film. A brief consideration of these developments will help to position *The Donna Reed Show* as a text that is a prime example of the Hollywood sitcom that emerged in the television industry in the 1950s.

The Sitcom from Radio to Television

While the notion of the situational comedy can be extended as far back as antiquity, the sitcom as we know it was initially a product of radio. After television arrived in 1948, producers looked to radio for programming ideas, with the hope that audiences would follow hit shows to television. Thus, many early television programs were originally on radio, which itself drew on the conventions of low cultural forms such as vaudeville, the music hall, and newspaper comics, as well as high cultural forms such as novels and theater. Many radio sitcoms, like early television, featured urban ethnic working-class families that were familiar to large immigrant populations in large cities. These were based on ethnic humor, broad stereotypes, and set comic pieces; in addition, their reliance on popular comedians already known for vaudeville acts helped create the self-reflexive backstage sitcom whereby comedians played fictionalized versions of themselves. *The George Burns and Gracie Allen Show,* for example, although not an ethnic comedy, was initially a vaudeville act that was brought to radio and then television; it starred comedians George Burns and Gracie Allen who played themselves, with Burns often breaking the fourth wall to directly address the audience. These rather unruly sitcoms, which typically emphasized comic performance over narrative verisimilitude, coexisted with more domesticated sitcoms that presented characters and situations in a humorous though realistic manner, such as *The Life of Riley* (1949–50; 1953–58), *The Goldbergs,* and *Mama.* These latter sitcoms eschewed self-reflexive techniques that broke the fourth wall in favor of realism built on audience identification. *The Donna Reed Show,* while tied to realism, retained traces of self-reflexivity by deliberately blurring the boundaries between Donna Reed and Donna Stone. Both had Mullenger as a maiden name, both came from Iowa, and Donna Stone was an amateur actress who had always dreamed of an acting career. Dream sequences feature Donna Stone appearing in scenes that evoke film genres, often playing the bad-girl roles that were denied to Donna Reed. In other cases, singers such as Tony Martin, James Darren, and Lesley Gore played themselves, and *The Donna Reed*

Show showcased professional athletes Willy Mays and Don Drysdale, who performed cameo roles. In another reflexive touch, Carl Betz played his own father whenever his dad appeared on an episode.

While ostensibly depicting ordinary life in a realistic manner, *The Donna Reed Show*, like some of the early self-reflexive television sitcoms adapted from radio, also acknowledged the artifice of the world portrayed on television. In the first season, occasional episodes end with the cast breaking into smiles to signify closure. Although the show was not filmed in front of an audience, the sound track simulates audience laughter and applause to convey a sense of liveness and immediacy. As Spigel (1992) notes, the major networks initially drew on the conventions of both legitimate theater and vaudeville for their programming. Television was believed to provide a sense of liveness, presence, and immediacy that was most similar to the experience of being at the theater. She writes that "According to the popular wisdom, then, television was able to reproduce reality in a way no previous medium could. Whereas film allowed spectators imaginatively to project themselves *into a scene,* television would give people the sense of being *on the scene* of presentation—it would simulate the entire experience of being at the theater" (139).

Early television audiences were already familiar with theatrical traditions from radio. Radio's live anthology dramas were based on theatrical productions, while the comedy-variety shows derived from vaudeville. Because television was perceived as closely akin to the experience of being at the theater, initially all of the networks favored live performances. Both the laugh track and the studio audience on sitcoms draw from this tradition. The simulated laughter and audience applause in single-camera sitcoms such as *The Donna Reed Show* is a remnant of this attempt to replicate the communal viewing experience of the theater, although its film style is far more cinematic than theatrical.

From New York to Hollywood

The domestic sitcom's shift in emphasis from vaudevillian-style comedy to narrative verisimilitude and from live performance to the telefilm was a consequence of Hollywood emerging as the locus of television production in the 1950s. In regard to the change in programming that occurred during this period, Boddy (1993, 1) writes that "prime-time programming also shifted from New York to Hollywood, from anthology programs to continuing-character series, and from the dramatic model of the legitimate theater to that of genre-based Hollywood entertainments." Both the television and film industries benefited from this change. By allowing Hollywood studios and independent film companies to produce programs, the networks were freed from the control of sponsors and assumed less financial risk associated with program development. For Hollywood, at a time when the B movies that had sustained the industry were being phased out, filmed television programs allowed them to maintain standardized studio-based production. Thus, as Hollywood film studios and independent producers began to make television programs, telefilms began to replace live programming, and sitcoms supplanted variety shows. According to Castleman and Podrazik (1984, 56) in reference to CBS and its programming strategies, "the network felt such programs could overcome some of the weaknesses of the variety format by presenting viewers with continuing characters, settings, and stories, rather than week after week of unrelated skits, which often looked like sixty minutes of random activity." While live television was standard in the early years of television, in the period from 1955 to 1959 the Hollywood film studios became the major suppliers of television programs, and by the end of the 1950s filmed television programs became the dominant product of the Hollywood studios and the dominant form of television programming (Anderson 1994, 7). In 1954, *Father Knows Best* became the first filmed sitcom made by a major studio, the Screen Gems division of Columbia Pictures, and provided a template for studio-produced middle-class domestic comedies such as *The Donna Reed Show.*

While the development of the telefilm—a television program that is filmed rather than live—is often credited to Desilu, the telefilm was emerging as an alternative to live television as soon as the film industry became involved in television production. Both *The Life of Riley* and *The Stu Erwin Show* (1950–55) were filmed sitcoms made before *I Love Lucy,* and both *Amos n' Andy* (1951–53) and *Dragnet* (1951–59) were telefilms that premiered the same year as *I Love Lucy. I Love Lucy,* the first filmed sitcom to become a national hit, is known among television historians for establishing the three-camera telefilm shooting style that became standard practice for sitcom production in later years. Desilu hired film cinematographer Karl Freund, who developed the idea of filming the show in front of a live audience using a multicamera setup that allowed the episode to be shot in real time. He also developed the uniform overhead lighting style, which enabled the three cameras to work simultaneously, and also disabled the use of lighting as expressive technique. The production techniques preserved the proscenium arch of theater while directing the television audience's point of view to different spaces. The use of three cameras also meant that a language of film different from classical Hollywood had to be developed, particularly as the use of three cameras did not allow for close-ups that had the same visual style as other angles (Landay 2010, 31). *I Love Lucy's* production practices provided the model for later multicamera sitcoms shot in front of a live studio audience.[1] *The Donna Reed Show,* in contrast, remained true to classical Hollywood and was a single-camera sitcom with no live audience, which accounted for its different aesthetic as compared to *I Love Lucy.*

While early television predominately consisted of urban ethnic or working-class sitcoms, such as variety shows, these virtually disappeared from the airwaves by the end of the

1950s. As production shifted from New York to Hollywood and as television became available nationwide, these were replaced by homogenous middle-class families. Even the remaining urban ethnic and vaudeville-based sitcoms demonstrated a marked turn toward a depiction of middle-class life. The shift was epitomized when *The Goldbergs* was renamed *Molly* in 1954 and the family moved from an apartment in the Bronx to a suburban house in Haverford, Connecticut. Similarly, *The George Burns and Gracie Allen Show* aired live in its first two seasons (1950–52) and incorporated musical numbers along with George Burns's stand-up comedy routine interspersed throughout each episode; by the time it left the air in 1958, it had largely become a conventional domestic sitcom that rarely broke the fourth wall. *The Adventures of Ozzie and Harriet* from the start emphasized character and story line rather than the vaudevillian performance that characterized the radio show. While it retained some self-reflexive aspects, largely because it was based on a real-life celebrity family, the on-screen Nelsons were wholesome paragons of middle-class virtues, and plots revolved around mundane, trivial problems that characterized their life in the suburbs. *The Donna Reed Show* too, while trading on the real-life image of its star Donna Reed who was ostensibly playing herself as a wife and mother, fictionalized her as the suburban Donna Stone.

The suburban domestic sitcom, first exemplified by the long-running *The Adventures of Ozzie and Harriet,* was the safest type of programming for both the networks and the advertisers as television expanded beyond the cities into the American heartland. On radio, bandleader Ozzie Nelson and his real-life wife Harriet played themselves in a program that bridged comedy-variety and sitcom. They had musical numbers and celebrity guests but also played themselves as a normal middle-class family raising their children in Hollywood. (Actors played the roles of the children until their real-life sons, Ricky and David, were old enough to take the parts.) When Ozzie Nelson decided to take the show to television in 1952, he retained almost complete creative control and wrote, produced, and directed almost every episode, although he hired a cinematographer to shoot episodes on film. The set was a replica of their real-life home, and as in radio, the entire Nelson family played themselves. But in the television version, the Nelsons lived in an unspecified typical American neighborhood rather than Hollywood, and they eliminated their wisecracking maid Gloria. Not only did this erase any trace of vaudeville-style comedy, but it also eliminated any suggestion that the Nelsons were other than middle class. In the television version, Ozzie's job was also unspecified. According to Nelson, "by not specifying the kind of work I did, people were able to identify with me more readily" (Jones 1992, 92). The innocuous Nelsons became the idealized American television family that came to characterize the domestic sitcom genre. Ozzie was always home, Harriet rarely complained, and the children were spirited but ultimately dutiful. *The Adventures of Ozzie and Harriet* was also, in a sense, one of the first reality shows. Viewers saw the Nelson children grow up on camera, and the savvy Ozzie used the program to launch the musical career of his son Ricky, a move that was mimicked by *The Donna Reed Show,* which manufactured singing careers for Shelley Fabares and Paul Petersen.

By the 1957–58 television season, just before *The Donna Reed Show* premiered, Hollywood had usurped New York as the television-production capital of the world, and the white middle-class suburban domestic sitcom shot on film became the dominant comedy form (Edgerton 2007, 179). There were no ethnic or racial groups other than white, there were no working-class families, and women became contented housewives whose husbands provided a steady hand. The domestic sitcom was an ideal form in which to advertise individual products, define the good life, and present the middle-class nuclear family as the core support for consumer culture. Situation comedies that featured suburban middle-class families both fulfilled an industry need and articulated ideals and aspirations for the postwar generation.

The Hollywood Sitcom

The Donna Reed Show, emerging just as the film industry became dominant in television production, exemplifies the Hollywood sitcom: a domestic comedy whose cinematic production styles and practices merge form and content to produce meaning. Like Hollywood films, they are shot with a single camera and include close-up shots, deep-focus photography, low-key lighting, and montage editing that relate narrative form and content for dramatic effect. These differ from what Barker (1985, 235), citing *Leave It to Beaver* and *My Three Sons* (1960–72) as examples, refers to as "1960s telefilm values," characterized by a utilitarian formulaic shooting style that almost never uses close-ups or creative performer blocking: "Programs produced with these 1960s telefilm values suggest that reinforcing the structure of the program narrative (e.g., the ebb and flow of conflicts) with particular production techniques was not a fundamental concern for the producers."

The Donna Reed Show was made using the production techniques borrowed from Hollywood film in order to allow for creative leeway in shaping the story during the editing process. After the cast rehearsed an episode, a number of master shots, medium shots, and close-ups were filmed over several days, though not in sequential order. In contrast to a multicamera sitcom such as *I Love Lucy* that required uniform high-key lighting, the use of a single camera allowed for expressive lighting and montage sequences created for dramatic effect. The show was filmed in a replica of a suburban home on the Columbia Pictures Ranch, a forty-acre lot in Burbank, California. The use of a "real" home rather than a stage allowed for deep-focus photography and layered action in foreground and background that contributed to its realistic feel. The houses were on Blondie Street, a facsimile of a suburban block whose twelve homes were later used in other Screen Gems sitcoms; for example, *The Donna Reed Show* house was the same one used in *Dennis the Menace* in 1959 and in the pilot episode of *The Partridge Family* in 1970. There were early examples of cross-promotion with other television characters: both Dennis the Menace and Lassie made appearances on *The Donna Reed Show.* In "Donna Decorates," Dennis the Menace helps (or hinders) Donna as she attempts to repaint the living room, and the episode ends with her making a desperate call for help to Mr. Wilson. "The Stones Go to Hollywood" (discussed in detail later in this chapter) concludes with the Stone family meeting a Hollywood celebrity, Lassie. Campbell's Soup sponsored *Lassie* in addition to *The Donna Reed Show.*

Caldwell (1995) writes at length about the structural function of visuality in early television as well as the way that television positioned itself in relation to film. He asserts that even when production moved to Hollywood, sitcoms largely distanced themselves from highly stylized cinematic techniques in favor of a straightforward, naturalistic style of storytelling. Desilu is a case in point. Desilu hired Karl Freund, one of Hollywood's best-known cinematographers who was famous for filming Fritz Lang's *Metropolis,* but none of Freund's expressionist style was evident in *I Love Lucy.* Caldwell refers to the result as "zero-degree television" (55).

Yet Caldwell (1995, 50) also states that "although many telefilms were bland, expressive lighting and choreographed cinematography were not uncommon in late-1950s television." He cites two episodes of *Father Knows Best* ("Hero Father" and "Formula for Happiness") as cases that displayed expressive cinematic techniques and asserts that formal experimentation is a little-known aspect of many of these television programs. *The Donna Reed Show,* because it was so imbricated in Hollywood film practices through its star, producers, directors, and writers, is the premiere example of the Hollywood sitcom that exhibits expressive cinematic aesthetics and values.

Several episodes of *The Donna Reed Show* incorporate the style and aesthetics of established film genres. "The House on the Hill," for example, employs the tropes of a gothic horror film to create an atmosphere of menace. There is no laugh track throughout the episode, in which Donna goes to visit a reclusive neighbor, Mrs. Allison, to ask for a charity donation. The horror film genre is signaled immediately: Donna opens rusty gates as she approaches a decrepit mansion, and there is a close-up of the wind blowing the second-floor shutters open, with thunder in the background. Eerie music plays as Donna gets out of her car, with shutters still banging in the wind. She walks to the door, and the camera zooms in to an elderly man dressed in a

48

This scene from "The Chinese Horse" uses expressive lighting to create a feeling of menace.

butler's suit who gazes at her from out of the upstairs window. Before Donna knocks, the creaky door opens seemingly on its own, and a maid peers out. Wordlessly, she allows Donna to enter. The house is candlelit, which casts heavy shadows, and cluttered with arcane objects. As Donna toys with a music box, Mrs. Allison, dressed in old-fashioned clothes, enters and yells, "Don't touch that!" Mrs. Allison orders Donna to sit. There is an alarming burst of music, and as Donna attempts to take a seat, Mrs. Allison shouts in alarm, "No not there!" The camera slowly pans up from a close-up of a pair of man's slippers on the floor to reveal that they are placed in front of an empty chair. Donna moves to another seat and states her purpose for the visit. Mrs. Allison seems more engaged in her solo game of tiddly winks but eventually tells Donna that she'll think about donating money.

"House on the Hill" made use of tropes from the gothic horror film.

The ominous mood continues. When Donna attempts to leave, the butler again observes her from the window as she walks to her car. When it won't start, he gives a nod of satisfaction. Donna is forced to return inside, where she observes Mrs. Allison conversing with "Alfred," who is represented only by the slippers and empty chair. Mrs. Allison then tells Donna she has no telephone, although one has appeared in an earlier shot, and tells the butler to go to the general store to call Donna's husband. The butler approaches the stairs, where he exchanges a glance with the maid, and he burns the piece of paper upon which Donna has written her number. They then inform Donna that the store is closed and that she will have to stay for dinner. Donna is trapped in the house, and as the butler takes her upstairs to freshen up, Mrs. Allison, shot in close-up, gazes slightly off camera and remarks, "She'll add something, Alfred," and with a wink to the camera she adds, "Don't you think?" She appears to be speaking to her dead husband, but she almost appears to be addressing the viewer. The episode continues as Alex arrives to find Donna but is sent away. Donna sees him from the window and bangs at it in vain. As she turns from the window and rushes downstairs, frantically calling "Alex!" over and over again, the music intensifies. The butler tells her that she was mistaken to think that Alex had been there and takes her to the dinner table. The table is set for at least twelve people, although only Donna and Mrs. Allison are there. The butler brings a bottle of champagne, and Mrs. Allison proposes a toast to "Alfred and all my dear departed friends, and to you my dear. Aren't you going to join us?" Donna sips her champagne quite nervously.

There is a happy ending tacked on to the episode. It is Mrs. Allison's fiftieth wedding anniversary, and the butler and the maid have detained Donna because Mrs. Allison hadn't left the house or interacted with anyone since she lost her husband twenty-five years earlier. Donna encourages Mrs. Allison to get out and live again, and of course Mrs. Allison donates money to Donna's cause. But throughout, the episode is determinedly not a sitcom. There are no jokes, and the episode depends upon viewers' knowledge of classic horror films: an isolated mansion, wind, thunder, eerie music, shadows, candles, creepy house-keepers, a somewhat imbalanced recluse, and a woman trapped inside. The episode plays with the classic horror form and in so doing brings a filmic aesthetic to television.

Episodes of other 1950s' sitcoms, such as *Ozzie and Harriet* and *Father Knows Best,* also incorporated film aesthetics and thus shared characteristics of the Hollywood sitcom as exhibited by *The Donna Reed Show.* The *Ozzie and Harriet* episode "An Evening with Hamlet," for instance, is distinguished not only by a heavy reliance on dissolves rather than the more conventional cuts to link scenes but also by a lengthy montage sequence that helps to create the unreal tone of the entire episode. The Nelsons' television set has broken, so they decide to spend the evening reading Hamlet. A mysterious stranger (played by John Carradine) rings the doorbell; he wears a long black cape and speaks in the sonorant tones of a trained Shakespearean actor. At first he says that he is lost, but when he learns that they are reading Hamlet he offers to instruct them, and as the episode proceeds Ozzie's poker buddies, along with the television re-pairman, join in. As each character recites lines from Hamlet, Elizabethan flute music plays, and the dissolves that link each character's reading are so slow that images are superimposed over one another so that a double image of each scene is read-ily apparent. The lengthy montage indicates time passing, al-though with a startling visual effect. At evening's end when the play is over, the stranger leaves and tells them that he was not lost but that he came because "I heard the voice calling . . . saw the sign you might say." Ozzie and Harriet are mystified until Ricky shows them a sign charging twenty-five cents admission to the play that Ricky had put in the front yard. There appears to be a neat resolution that reaffirms the narrative realism that marks the show until they see that the mysterious stranger has left a shilling on the table, which throws the neat resolution into question.

The characteristics of the Hollywood sitcom are especially apparent in dream sequences where visual excess erupts. The *Father Knows Best* episode "Betty Earns a Formal" is particularly illustrative. Betty wants to buy an expensive dress to impress her date. Despite her flirtatious wheedling (she tickles her father's arm as she pleads with him), Jim refuses. He later feels guilty and relents, but Betty rejects his help because she has taken a part-time job, although she will not reveal where. Her attempt at independence brings on new worries, demonstrated in an elaborate dream sequence. Jim twists and turns in bed, shot in medium close-up, and dramatic lighting casts shadows over him. A slow undulating dissolve indicates that he is dreaming, and suddenly Betty appears in a Western saloon called Red Devil. She is dressed primly and is trying to escape from the grasp of the saloon madam, who demands that Betty dance with the customers. Betty protests, saying "I didn't know it was this kind of a job!" The bartender guffaws, and as the woman pulls at Betty she calls for her father. He is visible outside the door of the saloon, still dressed in his pajamas. He bangs on the door and shouts "Let me in!" Another dissolve shifts him from dream to reality, and he finds that he is sleepwalking and is banging on the door of his bedroom closet. Jim can't distinguish between Betty finding a job and becoming a prostitute. Her independence is equated with her emerging sexuality, both of which threaten her father.

Here the visual excess of the dream reveals what is repressed in the domestic sitcom. In both *Father Knows Best* and *The Donna Reed Show,* sexuality is mainly present in the Other world of film. In the case of *Donna Reed,* dreams and fantasies also express Donna Stone's hostility toward her family and the demands they place upon her. The dream sequences disrupt narrative verisimilitude while demonstrating the churning undercurrents that trouble the text of the idealized nuclear family of the domestic sitcom.

Donna's Dreams: At the Interstices of Film and Television

While the Hollywood sitcom was clearly indebted to film, much early television was marked by ambivalence toward the film industry. In many television programs, the medium of television was associated with the home and ordinary people, while film was the realm of celebrity and excess. Caldwell (1995, 39–40) notes that the narratives of 1950s' family sitcoms, and *Donna Reed* in particular, often positioned art, film, and other forms of high culture as threats to suburban domesticity and the nuclear family.

"The Stones Go to Hollywood" is probably the episode that most clearly marks *The Donna Reed Show* at the interstices of film and television, as it plays with Donna Reed's image as the ideal mother who is also a Hollywood star and uses a dream sequence to contrast the domestic world of television versus the unnatural or unhomely world of film. The episode opens with a conventional narrative tableau. A deep-focus three-shot allows all members of the family to appear on screen at once. Donna and Jeff are in the foreground; Donna sits at the left end of the table sewing, while Jeff sits on the right doing his homework. Mary is in the background, talking on the phone about a new film being made called *Pepe*. Alex comes home and announces that he is traveling to Los Angeles to discuss the opening of a new children's clinic and invites the family to join him. Cut to stock footage of a plane landing and the exterior of a hotel with a sign that says "Hollywood," and then the Stone family is inside a hotel room, gazing out at the Hollywood Hills. The Stone family is not in Hilldale anymore. This is a special episode in which the family is placed outside of the familiar domestic confines of the program.

The Stones visit a movie set in "The Stones Go to Hollywood."

They make plans for how to spend the day while Alex is working, but rain prevents them from enjoying any of their planned activities, which include celebrity sightings. Alex returns to a bored family, who rejects his offer to attend a dinner party with his colleagues. They liven up, however, when they learn that George Sidney, the director of *Pepe,* is head of the hospital committee. They have already turned down his dinner offer, but they persuade Alex to call him to wrangle an invite to, in Mary's words, "A real studio with real stars!"

The episode is already a highly reflexive attempt to promote *Pepe,* a film in which Donna Reed was playing a cameo role at the time. (George Sidney, the director, had conducted her first screen test for MGM.) The studio lot that the Stones visit is the Columbia lot where *The Donna Reed Show* is shot, and they *are* the celebrities whom ordinary families would seek out in Hollywood. But in their ordinary dress, they contrast with the actors in costume: medieval soldiers, dancers wearing boas, and a hillbilly with a top hat. When the Stones enter Sidney's office, they see the back of a man dressed in a cowboy suit and later learn that he is Gregory Peck. Sidney teases them by listing the other movie stars they'd missed at dinner the night before, among them Lana Turner, Cary Grant, Doris Day, and Bobby Darin. When Sidney sees the Stones' crestfallen faces, he asks if they'd like to see him shoot a scene. They agree, at which point they (and viewers) are treated to a clip from *Pepe* in which two men wearing oversized sombreros dance in front of a life-sized telephone.

Here a surreal element is inserted into the narrative diegesis, but it is in Donna's dream that we see the cinematic play that marks the point of the exercise. When Mary confesses to Sidney that she is disappointed that they hadn't met any stars, he offers them a compensatory role as extras in the film and tells them that the shoot will take place the following day. That night both Alex and Donna are tense about their impending on-screen appearance, expressed through the interplay of shadows as they prepare to go to sleep. Donna is restless, and music begins as she leafs through the pages of a movie magazine. Her dream is signaled by an extremely long take of a close-up of her reclining head, in profile with eyes closed. The background is in soft focus, and the camera moves in. Just before dropping off she comments, "It's surprising how many movie stars have children." After Alex asks "What so surprising about that?" we see Donna's face in extreme close-up and in center frame, and she answers, "I don't know, I just never think of them having private lives." The framing here deliberately confuses Donna Stone and Donna Reed. Donna Reed is a movie star with children and a private life, while Donna Stone is the image of the ideal mother.

Donna's dream sequence is signaled by a slow dissolve of a close-up of her head with eyes shut. She awakens as a version of Bette Davis, complete with exaggerated, affected voice. In the dream sequence, Donna uses a cigarette holder, has dangly diamond earrings, and wears a sequined dress. Her life is presented as a cliché: her day is taken up with fan mail, press screenings, and interviews, and she sits signing autographed posters (of Donna Reed's publicity photo). She does not directly address her assistant but gazes into the mirror and adjusts her hair as she speaks. When her assistant asks her if she'd like to see her children, she answers, "What children?" She has to be reminded of their names. When they enter, they tell her that they wanted to see her because they'd forget what she looked like if they didn't see her movies. She dismisses them with copies of her autographed posters.

The scene plays on the camp images of narcissistic Hollywood stars and champions the ordinary, domestic Donna Stone while condemning the trappings of Hollywood celebrity and the glamorous life. Donna Stone, the movie star, then asks her assistant, "Why can't I be like other mothers and spend time with my children?" The response is, "That's the price you pay for being a star." Here motherhood is presented as incompatible with stardom. Donna then answers, "Well then it's not worth it. I want to be just simple Donna Stone: secure in the love of my husband and children. Oh, don't forget to tell the photographers to photograph me only on this side." The latter comment is an inside joke, as Donna Reed always asked directors to photograph her from the left, which she believed was more flattering.

George Sidney then enters the room and tells the movie star Donna that her latest film has grossed twenty-two million dollars. Like Donna Reed who pretended not to be a businesswoman, she at first protests that she doesn't know anything about facts and figures and then asks him questions that reveal her financial acuity. He offers her another film role, after which she tells him that she is giving up her film career to be a mother. He hands her a script (supposedly written by Ernest Hemingway). At first she refuses to accept it but then skims it and says, "I'll take it." Again this is a send-up of Donna Reed, who publically stated that she gave up film roles and went to television to be able to spend more time with her family but who was also not getting choice film offers. The episode ends soon after Donna Stone wakes up, realizes that it was all a dream, and smiles in relief.

In Freudian psychology, dreams represent an attempt to fulfill unsatisfied desires, and on one level this dream can be read as an expression of Donna Reed's wish for stardom. She is, after all, portrayed as a Hollywood diva, and this sequence allows her to fantasize about what her life could have been. In another sense, dreams often reveal what is forbidden, and here Donna Stone is allowed the sexuality that is absent from the domestic sitcom. The dream illuminates her character by highlighting the opposition between the domesticated, asexual television mother and the unmotherly but sexual star, and it does so in a way that seems to validate the domestic sitcom.

"The Stones Go to Hollywood" worked on a metalevel to criticize Hollywood excess while using highly stylized excessive film techniques in order to do so. The episode sets up a dichotomy between film and television in order to affirm television and its domestic values as well as to perpetuate Donna Reed/ Donna Stone's image as not a movie star but rather a mother. Even though Donna Reed was a film star with a career that took her away from her children, here Donna Stone's domesticity and contentment within the home is affirmed. Film and Hollywood are not domestic; movie stars must abandon their children for their careers, but television stars can be maternal. Television and television stars are familiar and comfortable; they are ordinary rather than excessive.

Throughout *The Donna Reed Show*, dream sequences mark the moment where television becomes cinematic, and the cinematic sequences reveal all of the tensions that television represses. The dreams manifest as a number of cinematic genres, from gangster film to Western to musical burlesque (making use of the film sets on hand), and their stylistic excess contrasts with the mundane world of the domestic sitcom. In "The Fatal Leap," for example, Donna and her friend Madeline spend a dull night together while their husbands attend a bachelor party. Madeline brings a library book that describes the debauchery of the male bachelor party. Later Donna falls asleep, and her dream becomes a burlesque musical with showgirls and can-can music. Alex whirls and twirls the dancers. With a look of anticipation on his face, he advances toward a huge cake from which a hand emerges but is taken aback when Donna is the slinky dancer who bursts out of the cake. In the dream, Donna Reed as Donna Stone interrupts and tames Alex's fantasy of wild abandon.

Similarly, "The New Look" plays on Donna Reed/Donna Stone's wholesome image by using Mary as a stand-in for Donna in two dream sequences that also emulate film genres. Mary complains that she is tired of being called wholesome and asks Donna to help her redefine herself. As Mary stares into a mirror, she decides that "I want to be flamboyant." After a wavy dissolve accompanied by music, Mary makes an entrance into a soda shop. She wears a tight form-fitting dress with a long sweeping scarf. She speaks in a southern accent and carries a parasol, which she spins as she breaks into dance. The soda shop becomes theater, and several boys perform an orchestrated dance with her, each swooning and falling as they gaze into her eyes. But Mary decides that this isn't right and returns to her mirror. Instead she wants to be "smoldering like a volcano." She then becomes a nightclub singer; she wears a long gown with elbow-length gloves, her hair is pinned up, and she speaks in a low sexy voice. This time, the boys are attracted to what she describes as her "inner conflict and turbulence," which is exactly what is repressed in the wholesome domestic sitcom. In the cinematic dream Mary is allowed to be sexual and complicated, but when she returns to her mirror, she is brought back to the safe world of domesticity that marks the television sitcom and away from the dangerous world of film. Donna assures Mary that what's most important is that she be herself. "Herself" is of course wholesome like Donna Stone, and the two are shot alongside one another so that they look virtually identical. Donna Reed has the final word, though. When Mary responds to Donna's advice with "Mother, you're the living *most*," Donna Reed/Donna Stone quips, "And all my life I wanted to be smoldering." Donna Reed acknowledges her desire to play the roles that Hollywood denied her.

Conflation of Film and Television in *The Donna Reed Show*

Because *The Donna Reed Show* was so closely aligned with film, its positioning of film as the immoral Other to television was inconsistent. The *Donna Reed Show* was just as likely to depict both film and television as allies unified in common opposition to high culture. Screen Gems first began broadcasting films on television in 1956, and "Boys Will Be Boys," which aired in 1959, revolves around a televised gangster film. Jeff and houseguest David Barker eat an entire chocolate cake and stay up late to watch an adult gangster film while Donna and Alex are out for the evening. In a remarkable sequence, there is an extreme close-up of the television set, and viewers see only the screen. For a full two minutes viewers watch the film, which is framed only by the rounded square of the television set, with only two brief cutaways to the boys. Viewers are effectively seeing an advertisement for films on television, which was a relatively new phenomenon at the time. Later, a guilty David tries to go to sleep and has a nightmare in which Alex is playing the gangster and Donna is playing his moll. *The Donna Reed Show* turns into a gangster film, and the viewers see the plot develop, with the Stone family as characters. Donna gets to play the villainess. She wears a slinky black dress and long diamond earrings, and she files her nails with what looks to be a weapon. She dominates the scene as she tries to get David to talk by threatening him with a bottle of truth serum topped with a long hypodermic needle. The nightmare does not end well. Donna (in her role as moll) sends David away, and as he departs Jeff and a boy from David's school, dressed in gangster attire, gun him down, which prompts him to awaken. Later Donna and Alex chastise the boys for their disobedience but not for watching a violent film, and indeed the choice of imagery in the nightmare sequence suggests that television violence is condoned rather than criticized. Both the gangster film on television and the nightmare sequence that advances its plot work to conflate film and television, further accented by the confounding of Donna Reed/Donna Stone as both film and television actress.

The positioning of film and television as popular forms of entertainment is even more apparent in "Nothing Like a Good Book." This episode addresses and allays concerns about the detrimental effects of media—especially television—that were circulating at the time. The following year, FCC chairman Newton Minow made his famous "Vast Wasteland" speech, partly in response to criticisms of the medium of television. The entire episode is a justification for popular entertainment over high culture and an assurance that ordinary people enjoy television as well as movies and rock and roll music. The episode begins with Donna mistakenly accepting a dinner invitation when "culture vulture" Lydia Langley calls while Jeff and Mary are warring over whether to watch television or listen to the record player, with each turning the volume up to make their point. Although the opening shot is a close-up of the record player, television is given prominence here: we see the large box and hear an advertisement for "Happy Gum," accompanied by an image of Jeff popping a piece in his mouth. Donna and Alex leave to escape the racket, and in the next scene at Lydia's house they are in the midst of a discussion about the merits of television. Lydia is the snobby, unlikeable representative of culture who asserts to the group that television is destroying the culture. Most of her guests are unresponsive, although a professor she is trying to impress rebuffs her and says only that it is influencing culture. He argues that "Attacking television is like attacking Gutenberg. You can't hold Gutenberg responsible for everything that appears in print." Here he is defending the medium, though perhaps not the message, as he equates its significance with the invention of the printing press. Lydia takes this opportunity to begin a discussion of books, which she believes are superior to television. A man asleep on the end of the sofa signifies the group's boredom. Lydia brags that her son is reading *David Copperfield* and tells the group that she is rereading *The Decline and Fall of the Roman Empire*. When Donna confesses that she hasn't read it, Lydia asks her about Tolstoy's *War and Peace*. The professor then chimes in that a movie of it has been made recently, although a woman in the group responds "Oh, movies," with disdain. The professor continues in his role as champion of ordinary culture as he asks Lydia if she has a television so he can see who won that night's fight. He, like the Stones, does not fit into this group of cultural elitists who do not care for film or television.

However, Donna is clearly shaken and the next day buys *David Copperfield* for Jeff, a Tchaikovsky record for Mary, and *War and Peace* for her and Alex to read together. Neither Jeff nor Mary are interested, and Alex tells a distraught Donna that you can't shove culture down their throats; you have to lead by example. She agrees and tells him that this is why they will read *War and Peace,* although Alex had planned to go bowling. This attempt at culture too is a failure (Donna can't pronounce the names of the characters), which prompts her to tell Lydia that they will join her book group. Lydia then demands that Donna report on *War and Peace* in two days. There is a montage of Donna reading while she's in bed, dusting furniture, baking a cake, sound asleep, and then again at the breakfast table in the morning. Even so, she doesn't get very far. At the book club,

Donna admits that she hasn't read the book and will never read the book. Alex then asks Lydia to give her interpretation. She begins but then falters and says, "The most dramatic scene in the book is when Audrey Hepburn and Mel Ferrar . . ." The group comes to life, and everyone begins reciting their favorite scene from the movie. In the end, they decide to play bridge rather than read books.

Movies trump literature, and even those with pretenses to high culture are secretly in their thrall. Ordinary people such as Donna Stone watch movies and television, and literature is a chore at best. This point is reinforced in the program's epilogue, when Jeff asks Donna if he can watch *Gunbutt*. When Donna asks Alex why Jeff wants to watch *Gunbutt* or why Mary wants to listen to rock and roll, he responds with "Why do we go all out for culture? It's because the other kids do." As if to underscore the message, Jeff then asks if two friends can join him, one who turns out to be the son of the culture vulture and purportedly spends all of his afternoons in the library. Alex asks Donna if she has ever watched the show. She says no, and he answers, "Well, how can we know what we're knocking? If you can't lick them, join them." They both sit down to watch television with Jeff and his friends. The final image is of the Stones and friends gathered around the television set, happily ensconced in a TV Western as the sound of gunshots fills the air. Television and film are naturalized as the activities of ordinary families, and cultural elitists who do not conform are out of touch with the real world.

More Trouble in the Text

Many episodes that import film styles and conventions to television, often through dream or fantasy sequences, are ways to speak the unspoken or to mark the trouble in the text. These sitcoms are marked by tensions and contradictions that are negotiated within the narrative. *The Donna Reed Show* subtly undermined the conventions of the domestic sitcom on the metatextual as well as textual level. The so-called woman's point of view that structured plotlines was often critical of postwar familial ideology, particularly with regard to gender relations. The episode "Three Part Mother" is an interesting example of both the aesthetics of the Hollywood sitcom and how those aesthetics convey the trouble in the text of *The Donna Reed Show*.[2] Like both the "Mama's Bad Day" episode of *Mama* and the "Molly's Dream" episode of *Molly* discussed earlier, "Three Part Mother" expresses Donna's resentment of the demands made upon her by her family. Rather than the complaints explicitly expressed in *Mama* or the dream sequence seen in *Molly*, Donna's voice-over narration conveys her internal thoughts. Silverman (1988) writes about the female voice in classical narrative cinema, arguing that sexual difference is conveyed through sound as well as image, and that the authorial voice, which conveys authority, typically belongs to a male. According to Silverman, "it has gone largely unnoticed that like the visual *vraisemblable,* the sonic *vraisemblable* is sexually differentiated, working to identify even the *embodied* male voice with the cinematic apparatus, but always situating the female voice within a hyperbolically diegetic context" (45). The female narrator, with its implications of authority and control, was as rare in 1950s' television as it was in classical cinema. In "Three Part Mother," Donna Stone's narrative voice attempts to disavow the tensions that mark the diegesis rather than convey the truth, and it is the gap between word and image that reveals the trouble in the text.

After the opening credits, there is a conventional establishing shot of the Stones' house. The camera zooms in and dissolves to the interior of the bedroom, an opening that is itself a departure from the zero-degree style that Caldwell (1995) describes. The shot brings us from a position outside the narrative into the private space of Donna and Alex Stone at the center of the story. We see Donna and Alex asleep in their twin beds; the alarm clock rings, and Donna grudgingly turns it off. In a voice-over we hear Donna's thoughts: "The man who invented alarm clocks must have hated people." She rises and sighs. Alex remains immovable, and her voice-over indicates a slight degree of irritation: "Why am I the only one who hears it?" However, her annoyance disappears when she nudges Alex. We hear "Now husbands, that's a nice invention" as we see them wink affectionately at one another. Donna's voice-over remains blissful as she begins her morning ritual of waking the family; she describes each of her wonderful children as she rouses them from slumber. When she returns to the bedroom, Alex has fallen back to sleep. Although her voice-over exudes sympathy for the late-night hours of a doctor on call, she rips the covers off him (the disjuncture between word and image prompts the laugh track). She nibbles at his ear (rather erotically) to finally rouse him. At the end of the scene, with her task done, an exhausted Donna falls onto her bed.

The opening narration sets the tone for the rest of the episode, which addresses the conflict between Donna's desire to be the perfect wife and mother and her resentment of what this requires. Throughout, Donna does physical and emotional maintenance on the family as she becomes increasingly distraught. At breakfast, she hovers at the stove while the family has their heads buried in the newspaper. They are connected to the outside world, while she is at work serving them. She expresses her resentment with sarcasm: "Well, don't move," she tells them. "Just cut holes in the paper so I can serve the eggs." Alex is preparing to give a talk, Jeff is excited about his basketball game (Donna unknots his Converse sneakers, which are prominently displayed), and Mary is getting initiated into a social club. Donna expresses her frustration when all three tell her that they want her to attend their event, and the plot revolves around how she will manage to satisfy everyone. She grows increasingly frustrated. When a friend of Alex's tells her to "wear something attractive, but nothing the wives will consider overdressed," she responds with an acerbic "I might wear a bikini with long white gloves." As the episode proceeds with the family's escalating demands that Donna be in three places at once, she cannot cope. She retorts, "I hope you all have a lovely time tonight. As for me, I'm getting into my toreador pants and going out to shoot billiards!" Instead, she retires to bed. She is shot center frame in medium close-up as she reclines comfortably, eating chocolates and leafing through a fashion magazine. The family enters her room to apologize. We expect her to acknowledge their repentance, but instead she tears up, nods at the children, and after a pause replies, "Alex, take them out of here." Quickly we hear her disavow any malicious intent in her remark as she voices her thoughts aloud: "Why did they have to be so sweet?" Here the disembodied narrator's voice from the opening becomes literally embodied as Donna expresses her thoughts, a move that mitigates her already tenuous narrative authority. Silverman (1988, 53–54) asserts that the narrator whose voice reveals an internal monologue—an embodied narrator who is not temporally distant from the story but interior to the diegesis—is least authoritative and in Hollywood films is equated with discursive impotence and lack of control. The narrative movement is to repress her discontent and shift back to the contented state initially evoked—if unconvincingly—by the opening narration, but it can only do so by having the narrator's voice disappear and meld into the story. As Donna loses her position as narrator, the voice of the contented mother she wishes she was takes control of the diegesis. She is recuperated back into the family and ends up attending, miraculously, all three events in the nick of time. She gets to Alex's speech in time to hear him recommend in all seriousness that mothers be given sedatives in order to allay their children's anxieties about their first pediatrician's visit.[3] As the episode concludes, she is framed tightly in the interior of the home as she closes her eyes to sleep at day's end. She hears a cacophony of voices calling "Mother," "Mom," and "Donna" and smiles peacefully as the screen fades to black. Narrative control, in the end, has been handed over to her family. They have the last word, even in Donna's unconscious, and Donna is once again confined to the inside of the home and the diegesis. Yet whether the figure is Mama, Molly, or Donna Stone, the reassuring image of the contented housewife does not convincingly allay the tensions that comprise the bulk of the narrative.

"Three Part Mother" was a first-season episode. "Author, Author," made during the eighth and final season of the show, demonstrates that tensions around gender and familial relations had not been allayed in succeeding years. Barbara Avedon wrote this episode, which may account for its sensibility. Avedon, the writer and cocreator of *Cagney and Lacey*, was both a feminist and a political activist not averse to using mainstream images and icons to make a political point. She founded the antiwar group Another Mother for Peace in 1967 along with Donna Reed, and their first action was to send Mother's Day cards that protested the Vietnam War to members of Congress. In 1966 as the women's movement was gaining force in American culture, the seeds of women's liberation could be seen in Avedon's writing for *The Donna Reed Show*.

A running theme throughout *The Donna Reed Show* was that the men in the family would scoff at Donna's abilities, and she would set them straight. This theme was evident as early as season 1, when in "The Hike" Donna decides to take Jeff and his friends camping when Alex is unexpectedly called to work. Despite Alex's skepticism she manages to make it work, although unbeknownst to Alex and Jeff she solicits the help of park rangers to set up the tent and has hunter's stew brought in rather than cooking it herself. In "Author, Author," Jeff and Alex's skepticism toward Donna's abilities is even more hostile and overt. Jeff gives Donna an aptitude test and learns that she has literary talent. Both Alex and Jeff smirk at the news and belittle her. Alex remarks, "Literary ability? As a matter of fact she does have a certain talent for letter writing. She turned out a masterpiece the other night—a note to Trisha's teacher. All about sniffles." Alex and Jeff guffaw, and Jeff replies, "I didn't believe it either. But I went over it three times." Donna is affronted, and later when she has coffee with her friend Midge, Midge encourages her to take up writing (although it must be said here that Midge too is skeptical of Donna's talent). Donna says that she is going to clean the attic instead, putting her housewifely duties ahead of her ambitions. She happens to find a typewriter in the attic, just as Midge brings her a book on artistic inspiration. They decide that she will write to show those "doubting Thomases" but that she must work in isolation and keep it a secret. Both literally and metaphorically, she needs a room of her own.

The tension between work and family is apparent when Alex comes home and there is no dinner. He picks up a pot and turns it upside down as he asks Jeff where Donna/dinner is. When Donna appears, she suggests that they go out to dinner, although Midge saves the day by bringing over a casserole because Donna "was too busy to cook today." This causes some consternation, and Jeff asks, "Busy doing what?" He then adds, "I thought she'd be busy writing the great American novel." Both women stop and gasp, giving it all away. Later, Alex and Jeff try to imagine what she is writing. They sit playing cards while Donna performs her neglected domestic duties by going to the grocery store. After she leaves they determine that she must be working in the attic, and the entire family rushes upstairs to invade her privacy and read her work.

As Alex begins to read Donna's description of him, the scene shifts to a fantasy sequence. There is a long dissolve, and Donna's words replace Alex's as we hear "The king of the household who in his spare time just happens to be a doctor was as usual entrenched and enthroned with the evening paper." We see Alex with his head buried in the paper, ignoring everyone around him. She continues to read her story in voice-over: "At last, not wanting to bother the head of the house, but in great need of help, she asked sweetly and got the usual answer."

There is a close-up of Donna smiling pleasantly, while Alex, looking stern, puts down the paper and is shot in a wide-angle distorted close-up as he responds with a lionlike roar. There are similar fantasy sequences in which Trisha exaggerates her cold so that she does not have to go to school and Jeff refuses to clean his room despite Donna's pleading. There is a final fantasy sequence in which Donna repeats the scene where Jeff revealed the results of the aptitude test, and we see the entire family laughing at her in exaggerated fashion.

Apart from when Donna is writing, throughout the episode she bustles about sewing, writing grocery lists, doing the shopping, and serving food to her family. But her writing and the fantasy sequences that portray her point of view illustrate the discontent shared by many housewives in the 1950s and 1960s. She is a domestic servant who is not taken seriously by her family or friends. She is resentful of a husband who pays her little attention after doing "real" work outside the home and of sick and sloppy children who take her for granted. She has no private space. They can't imagine that she would be busy doing anything other than domestic activities, and they think nothing of reading her work even though they know she is trying to keep it secret. There is a truth to her fantasy, although not one that is often apparent on *The Donna Reed Show*. The episode resolves with the family realizing the error of their ways: Alex helps her with the groceries, Trisha tells her that she is well enough to go to school, and Jeff cleans his room. In the end, the objective of Donna's writing seems to be to manipulate her family rather than to express herself or to find pleasure in the activity. Donna's literary aspirations are subordinated to her domestic concerns. Domestic harmony is restored, and the typewriter can once again gather dust in the attic. But the specter of dissatisfaction and disharmony has been raised, even if it is put to rest at the episode's end.

The Donna Reed Show and Domestic Melodrama

Nina Leibman, in *Living Room Lectures: The Fifties Family in American Film and Television* (1995), distinguishes between the depictions of family life in sitcoms of early television and in studio-produced domestic sitcoms that followed. Her distinction also helps differentiate between the Hollywood sitcom that emulates film melodrama and urban ethnic working-class sitcoms with roots in radio and vaudeville:

> Before 1954, television's depiction of family life could hardly be classified as contemporary domestic melodrama. Either the families depicted were working class (*The Life of Riley, The Honeymooners*) or urban (*The Danny Thomas Show*), or the shows themselves were star-based situational comedies (*I Love Lucy, Burns and Allen*). Regardless of configuration, the shows' narratives were traditional situation-comedy in which characters were victims of confusion and complication, jokes were broad and even slapstick, and verbal wordplay and performance were central. While these programs did provide a context and a foundation for the series which followed, they lacked an emphasis on familial love and relationships, moral transgressions, and lessons learned that was to come with the studio-produced family melodramas of the mid-to-late-50's. (7)

Leibman (1988) argues that domestic sitcoms such as *The Donna Reed Show* are more aptly characterized as melodramas than as comedies, particularly because of their reliance on emotional appeals and because there is always a moral lesson at the end. She writes that "if it was not for the presence of a laugh track, it would be difficult to classify these programs as 'comedies,' so replete are they with anxiety, despair, and complication" (25).

Most importantly, there was a level of irony that rendered them less ideologically cohesive than they first appeared. *The Donna Reed Show,* because it ostensibly put the mother front and center stage, is particularly complicated with regard to its lessons regarding gender and the family, and it can often be read through the lens of irony. While gender will be discussed in detail in the following chapter, here I will describe the melodramatic characteristics that trouble the text of *The Donna Reed Show.*[4]

Verbalization of repressed emotions. Melodrama involves the breaking through of repressed emotions to reveal one's true feelings and desires. In "Author, Author," for example, Donna's representations of her family, expressed in the fantasy sequence, reveal her innermost emotions. These "emotional breakdowns" are often linked to the central moral conflicts of the show, which in this case express Donna's resentment that her family takes advantage of her and does not take her seriously. Dream sequences are also a way to articulate repressed emotions, and in "The Stones Go to Hollywood," we see Donna's "forbidden" desire for fame and celebrity rather than the more mundane business of motherhood, although the moral of the story presents this desire as unnatural. In "Three Part Mother," Donna's voice-over attempts to disavow the anger and resentment toward her family that is apparent in the narrative, but her emotions break through, culminating in an outburst that sends her to bed. Although the end reaffirms her contentment, the contradictions remain unresolved.

Peripety, or a sudden reversal of events. According to Leibman (1995), reliance on peripety, defined as uncanny surprise or coincidence, is often what gives melodrama its unrealistic aura while providing its emotional appeal. The ringing of the doorbell or telephone often signals the coincidence that provides either narrative complication or resolution. In *The Donna Reed Show,* a close-up of the telephone is the first image in the opening credits; its ring brings Donna downstairs and sets the series in motion. Throughout the series, it is common for the phone, located in the center of the set where the x and z axes meet, to ring at inopportune moments with a message that Alex must go to the hospital for an emergency so that Donna is left in charge of whatever situation emerges. In other cases, as in "Nothing Like a Good Book," a phone call is the vehicle that causes misunderstandings that motivate the plot, or it is a phone call that ultimately resolves problems and dilemmas.

Music as emotional punctuation and structural cue. Music is used to highlight strong emotions, the point where a moral lesson is learned, where sentimentality exists, or where there is a narrative resolution. In *The Donna Reed Show,* the theme song "Happy Days" plays whenever there is a shift from humorous moments to those that illuminate emotional truth or provide catharsis. For example, music signals both the dream sequence in "The Stones Go to Hollywood" and the transition to Donna's voice-over in "Author, Author"; both of these sequences reveal Donna's inner thoughts and state of being. It is also a means to indicate the resolution of conflict, and it is often when we get a moral resolution that the theme music will play in the background. When "Three Part Mother" concludes with Donna falling off to sleep, we hear the theme music in the background, reinforcing the overt lesson of the show that a family's love trumps all the conflicting demands made on the mother.

Critical distantiation. There is a level of irony in melodrama in that it is a form whereby social institutions such as the family are both affirmed and critiqued. Thus, while programs often conclude with the restoration of family unity and harmony, the resolution is often undercut by the preceding narrative tensions. While "Nothing Like a Good Book" ends with the Stone family capitulating to the pleasures of television, they have also shown a desire to become more erudite that they cannot fulfill. "The Stones Go to Hollywood" self-consciously plays on the contrast between Donna Reed as movie star and Donna Stone as the ideal mother so that its resolution that affirms the value of motherhood over stardom is not entirely convincing. "Three

Part Mother" concludes with Donna smiling contentedly as she drifts off to sleep, yet the preceding half hour has shown her overwhelmed and frustrated at the family's demands for her time and attention. Similarly, "Author, Author" resolves with the family capitulating to Donna's wishes, but we have already seen her resentment and anger toward their everyday behavior.

Perhaps because the mother rather than the father is central to the narrative, throughout *The Donna Reed Show* there is a great deal of irony and self-conscious play that is crucial to melodrama. While Donna Stone is careful to play the role of the domestically contained 1950s' housewife, there is a critique that seeps through, partly through self-conscious play with the image and partly through the ways that she chafes at her familial responsibilities and yearns for something more. Episodes lend themselves quite easily to the double reading that is characteristic of irony, and this renders *The Donna Reed Show* less ideologically cohesive than might appear to be the case.

Donna Stone and the Feminine Masquerade

Throughout the 1950s and into the 1960s, domestic sitcom melodramas such as *The Donna Reed Show* provided an idealized vision of suburban life to a newly formed middle class. As mentioned previously, 1950s' domestic sitcoms largely worked to reconstitute the nuclear family in the postwar period by depicting male centrality and authority while positioning women as contented housewives who provided love and support. Leibman (1995, 173–218) writes that these sitcoms shared a common narrative structure characterized by the centrality of family and family issues, an omnipotence placed upon the family unit as the site of both problem and solution, and an emphasis upon the father as the means for a successful narrative resolution. She argues that in programs such as *Leave It to Beaver, Father Knows Best,* and even *Donna Reed,* the father-child relationship was valorized, even though the mother was home all day with the children. The title *Father Knows Best,* for example, exemplifies the role of the father as unquestioned head of household. However, *The Donna Reed Show,* while seeming to conform to this model, was able to offer an alternative image of the sitcom mom.

Leibman (1995) suggests that domestic sitcoms were a regressive cultural reaction to the increasing empowerment of women in terms of their independence during the war and the subsequent formation of the women's movement and the emerging idea of equality in the late 1950s. Yet while popular media extolled the virtues of motherhood, there was also an antimaternal strain, initiated by the fear of the attentive, overprotective mother whose constant presence exacerbated her influence over her children. The fear of so-called Momism was expressed in influential books such as Philip Wylie's *Generation of Vipers* (1942), which argued that American males were excessively attached to their mothers and that as a result they were becoming weak and unproductive. In middle-class domestic sitcoms, one cultural response to the perceived threat of the powerful mother and its flip side, the emasculated male, was to show the housewife as superfluous, unnecessary, or subordinate. It was not uncommon to see June Cleaver perched on the arm of a chair, listening but having no opinion of her own, while Ward dispensed advice to the boys. Ward served as moral arbiter and enforced discipline, even though June was home with the boys all day. June was frequently befuddled and needed to have Ward explain the boys' behavior to her, or in lieu of Ward, Wally would explain Beaver's behavior. In "Ward's Golf Clubs," for example, she keeps hearing noises as Beaver attempts to hide Ward's broken golf club until he can get it fixed. "What is that noise, Wally?" she repeatedly asks. And instead of investigating, she accepts his multiple versions of "I didn't hear anything." Even when Ward discovers Beaver's subterfuge and has dispensed him to the den for a lecture, June turns to Wally and asks in puzzlement, "Did this have anything to do with the door slamming before?" He dismisses her with "What would make you think that?" as he strides into the kitchen, effectively ending the conversation.

The Donna Reed Show was in all likelihood a more accurate reflection of the dynamic in most homes where the father was at work for most of the day, although this did not fit with postwar ideology that positioned the father at the center of the family. Donna Stone challenges the dominance of the sitcom father by presenting an image of a mother who "knows best." She is the disciplinarian in *The Donna Reed Show*, and she is rarely confused by her children's behavior. In "The Punishment," for example, Donna grounds Mary and Jeff for the weekend, which makes them angry. She becomes upset when they greet Alex with hugs and affection at the end of the day, and she thus insists that Alex become the disciplinarian. Not only is he incompetent at meting out punishments, but the children quickly become aware that Donna is giving him a list of behaviors to criticize, whereby she remains the power behind the male mouthpiece. But lest she appear too severe and patriarchal authority is questioned too strongly, at the end she relents and recants the punishment.

Leibman (1995) writes that Margaret Anderson of *Father Knows* was a slightly more developed character than June Cleaver. Unlike June, Margaret occasionally chafes at her domestic subjugation, such as in "Brief Holiday," when she takes a day off from the family, or in "Margaret Wins A Medal," when she enters a fishing contest because she is the only family member who has never won a trophy. In "Margaret Disowns Her Family," Jim mocks her attempt to write a classified ad, and then the children leave the house a mess. When daughter Kathy asks Margaret if she is going to disown the family, she replies, "There are moments . . ." But when Margaret realizes that Kathy has conveyed her discontent to a visitor who is herself dubious about marriage, Margaret quickly intervenes: "I know of nothing more worthwhile than a family. Oh, you can get irritated picking up your boy's jacket a thousand times, but what if you didn't have that boy to pick up a jacket for? You can get a little mad at your husband for barricading himself behind his newspaper at the breakfast table, but you just try eating breakfast without him there." The episodes reveal tensions but conclude with Margaret reaffirming her commitment to the family.

This is not unlike the narrative structure of *The Donna Reed Show,* in which tensions are brought up in the narrative and then are disavowed in the resolution. But in *Father Knows Best,* Margaret rarely controls the narrative, and thematically she is often incidental to the plot that revolves around the father-child dynamic. In "Betty Earns a Formal" (discussed in chapter 2), Betty negotiates her request for a dress with her father and ignores her mother, and the plot revolves around his feelings of guilt after he denies her. Margaret seems to have no opinion. When Jim has his nightmare and bangs on the closet door, it is Betty, rather than Margaret, who runs to his rescue. Betty bursts into the bedroom to ask what is wrong, and Margaret stands in the background while Jim and Betty discuss the dream. Margaret's only role is to tuck Jim into bed and ask him, "Would you like me to get you some warm milk?" It is also Jim whose machinations resolve the plot. He discovers that Betty is selling peaches in the local supermarket in order to earn enough money for her dress. He secretly buys several cases so that she reaches her mark, thus surreptitiously undermining her efforts to become independent and reassuring himself that he is still needed.

Donna Stone has a more complicated relationship to gender politics than June Cleaver or Margaret Anderson. In later years, those who had worked with Donna Reed considered her a feminist, and she once remarked that "My TV series certainly aggravated men. Hollywood producers were furious that Mom was equal and capable" (Fultz 1998, 132). But within the context of the show, she worked within the confines of the generic and societal expectations of a woman's place. Although Donna Stone's resentment of her role as housewife and her need to break free of her domestic constraints occasionally provide the dramatic tension that motivates the plot, she also dutifully returns to the family fold by the end of an episode. Unlike the other domestic sitcoms, however, we get Donna Stone's point of view and share experiences from her perspective. She adopts the masculine position of narrative control, but the threat that this imposes is negated by her femininity and her role as the "perfect" mother.

Femininity as Masquerade

One of the most fruitful ways to observe the character of Donna Stone, especially as she serves as a stand-in for Donna Reed, is to consider the concept of femininity as masquerade that was first proposed by Joan Riviere (1929 [1986]) and then adapted by theorists such as Steven Heath (1986) and Mary Ann Doane (1982). While Riviere's original concept referred to women who disguised their intellect through excessive displays of femininity, film theorists such as Heath and Doane use the concept to refer to women who violate social codes by occupying positions of authority typically ascribed to men. They wear a mask of extreme femininity in order to compensate for their "theft" of masculinity (Doane 1982, 82). It is important to note that this mask constructs their identity and does not disguise an essential identity beneath the mask. Donna Stone often acts as the head of the household; in a frequent plot device, she adopts Alex's role when he is called away on emergencies. She is shrewder than her husband, who is often outwitted by Donna's ploys. But the feminine excesses of her behavior—her physical appearance, her devotion to family meals and housework, and her overall complicity with the social codes and narrative constraints that demand that she accept her assigned role—often disguise the masculine position of authority that she occupies throughout much of the narrative.

Many episodes explore the tension between Donna's performance of femininity and her desire to break free of its constraints. It is along these lines that Heller (1995, 47) writes that Donna Reed's performance "seems to border on a kind of camp performance—a self-consciously stylized surrender to the social script, a script held in quotation marks by Donna's very insistence on acting it out with a kind of excessive sincerity that never precludes ironic undercuts or wry quips, often at the expense of her character." She is masquerading as feminine, excessively displaying the signs of contented domesticity, and in so doing she avoids being recognized as a powerful female who is challenging the social codes of the 1950s. In "The Ideal Wife," for example, which exhibits a great deal of self-conscious play with Donna Stone's/Donna Reed's public image, she resists being referred to as "sweet" and "perfect" by friends, family, and even the dry cleaner. This is an episode that depends on viewers having no memories of past episodes when Donna routinely chastises both the children and Alex and is anything but sweet. The episode plays with the idea of femininity as masquerade by having Donna contest her reputation as perfect wife and mother. The plot unfolds when the Stones host a dinner party and Donna reacts sympathetically after Alex is called out on an emergency. The female dinner guests, who are also doctors' wives, shower her with compliments for being so patient and "perfect." Here we see how Donna Stone uses a quip or barb to undercut her idealized image, though always ostensibly in jest. One of the women makes reference to Donna's even temper by commenting that "Any mother who can get through a day with children without screaming is a saint." Donna immediately deadpans, "I don't believe in screaming. A rubber hose is just as effective, and it doesn't leave marks." The next day, Mary and Jeff ignore Donna's requests to do chores but tell her that she is sweet. Alex asks her to go downtown and pick up his X-rays "within the hour," and then the dry cleaner arrives and praises Donna's amiable disposition. He comments, "You know what I always say to the Missus. If your house burned down, or worse yet, if your husband ran off with another woman, you'd still have a smile on your face." Donna tartly replies, "You know, today I think I would." She then decides that she will no longer allow people to take advantage of her, starting out with the unsuspecting dry cleaner, whom she makes return to the shop for a skirt he has forgotten to bring. Emboldened by her own assertiveness, she then loses her temper with Mary and Jeff and insists that they do their chores, and she puts her wishes ahead of Alex's and tells him that she would rather see a play than attend a work dinner where the host plans to screen a gall bladder operation. Alex assures the children that their mother is behaving "abnormally" and is puzzled that she seems to feel justified. Donna gets the results she desires: Mary and Jeff do their chores, Alex decides to take her to see *Death of a Salesman* after all, and the dry cleaner treats her with respect. However, she cannot maintain her new image as an assertive, if less than perfect, wife and mother. Just as she initially took her frustration out on the hapless dry cleaner, she quickly apologizes to him for being too demanding and informs him that even though she took a stand, she lost something too. She repents and resumes her masquerade as an accommodating wife and mother: she makes Alex his favorite dinner, buys Mary a new cardigan, and returns Jeff's allowance. Alex's relief is palpable as he tells Mary and Jeff, "The revolution is over and the people can return to their peaceful lives." Donna's "revolution" is short-lived; despite exerting her power in ways that make her less of a domestic servant, by the episode's end she willfully embraces her femininity and conforms to the expectations of others. However, viewers have seen her drop her sweet socially sanctioned masquerade, which does not entirely negate the rather pat ending that mitigates the threat posed by her self-assertion.

In season 4's "A Woman's Place," Donna runs for town council and neglects her family in the frenzied whirl of activity surrounding the campaign. This prompts Alex to have an anxiety dream that eventually she becomes mayor, governor, and then president. The experience is emasculating; in his dream a reporter asks him, "How does it feel to be the First Lady?" Alex gives a televised tour of the White House, in direct imitation of Jackie Kennedy's television appearance the year before. He wakes up and tells Donna, "I'm tired of losing my buttons, I'm sick of eating leathery eggs and carbon toast, and I'm sick and tired of being the First Lady of the land. . . . We need you more than the country does." Sentimental music plays in the background as Donna asks, "Say that again—that you need me." Alex hugs her close and says, "At least that's settled. Now all you have to do is concentrate on being a wife." Watson's (2008, 66) analysis of this episode states that "The moral of the story is that a woman has no business trying to make a difference in the world and that a man is justified in feeling diminished by the success of his spouse." Yet the show raises the possibility of a married woman running for office, which was highly unusual in 1962. It was not that Donna was incompetent or unenthusiastic, but her capitulation in the end was necessary to satisfy the narrative demand for stasis and to conform to the ideology of domestic containment.

80

A season 2 episode, "Career Woman," explicitly addresses the tension between working women and housewives. Donna's high school friend Molly, now an internationally known fashion designer, visits Donna. There is also a sense in which the episode contrasts the glamorous life of the film actress and the domesticity of the television mom, as Esther Williams, a well-known film actress and good friend of Donna Reed's, plays Molly. The contrast between the two is highlighted as Molly arrives in a mink coat while Donna is vacuuming, wearing an apron. Molly is unsure about whether or not to marry and fears a life of routine domesticity. As the two women sit before the fire and reminisce, she asks Donna, "Whatever happened to your dream of becoming the world's greatest actress?" (a nod to Donna Reed). Donna replies dutifully, "No regrets. Not since I met Alex. I think that was the real dream I had all along." Yet the word "sacrifice" occurs repeatedly throughout the episode. "If you marry David you'll have to resign yourself to be a season behind in waistlines," Donna remarks when Molly notices that Donna's coat is out of fashion. "If that were the only sacrifice I'd have to make, I'd make it," Molly replies. Yet by the end of the episode, Molly is in the kitchen wearing an apron and learning to cook. After observing the Stone family, she decides that the sacrifice is worth it and opts to surrender her career for the joys of marriage. But the blurring of Donna Reed and Donna Stone works both ways, and the audience knows that "Donna" did not sacrifice her theatrical aspirations, and the fashionable Donna Stone in her cinch-waist dresses is not "a season behind in waistlines." Even Molly's "surrender" to domesticity is unconvincing: she learns to cook but gets a blister and is clearly incompetent in the kitchen. When her fiancé arrives, he is hesitant to accept that she is ready for marriage. "With Molly it's a mood," he says. "She's just been exposed to the warmth of a family. There are other aspects of marriage." Donna tries to convince him that Molly is sincere but is not exactly selling the idea: "Oh David, Molly knows about the other things—sameness, routine, sacrifices. We haven't spared her the unglamorous side of marriage." It ultimately takes some reverse psychology whereby the Stones declare that Molly "doesn't have the qualities of a good wife" to get David to come to her defense, and he asserts that he wants to marry her not because of her domestic skills but because of her imagination and independence. Despite this celebration of unconventional attributes in a housewife, there is a conventional ending, although not one that is an unmitigated advertisement for marriage or that promotes the mask of the docile homemaker.

One of the most illuminating episodes with regard to the show's developing feminism that subverts the feminine masquerade is "Just a Housewife," in which Donna takes issue with the way that the word "housewife" demeans women. The episode begins in the supermarket, where a radio show host interviews women for a show called *Housewives Corner* and turns every comment into an opportunity to belittle the women who answer his questions. Donna bristles as he asks a Mrs. Burns what she does and she replies modestly, "I'm just a housewife." Donna whispers to a friend, "Did you ever notice how women seem to apologize when they say that?" Later Donna complains

Donna Stone in her apron contrasts with her friend Molly, a fashion designer, in "Career Woman."

to Alex, who tries to convince her that it is just a descriptive word. Like the radio talk show host, Alex is also demeaning as he asks incredulously, "Are you saying that you object to keeping house?" Donna answers, "It isn't that I object to doing housework. I just don't want to be known as just a housewife." Alex then dismisses her and other women who fought for women's rights: "I had a grandmother who used to handcuff herself to lampposts, and now, Maharani of the Mop, don't you think it's time to start dinner?"

Mary and Jeff then join in the discussion, with Jeff offhandedly referring to women as nags and with Mary taking Donna's side against men who don't take women seriously. "You start a serious discussion with a boy, and he acts as if you should be home baking a cake," Mary observes. The gender division is exaggerated here by two-shots of the women alternating with two-shots of the men as they talk. Alex continues to belittle Donna, telling the children, "From now on please address your mother as 'Princess of the Pantry.'" The conversation continues at dinner, and Donna's revenge is to tell Mary to leave the dishes for the men. In fact, Donna decides that Alex and Jeff will do the dishes for a whole week to see what it feels like to be "just a housewife." Alex asks in alarm, "You didn't really mean what you said about the dishes, did you?" Here we see the assumption of male power and privilege, even more so the following day when Donna is busy vacuuming and Alex enters the room and asks, "Darling, do you have any coffee ready?" She is affronted by the use of the label "housewife" but not by the domestic chores she is expected to complete, and she happily pours him a cup of coffee. After a faux pas when Alex offends Donna because he refers to another woman as "just a housewife," he states in exasperation, "Now I know you are sensitive to the word, but how else do I describe someone who stays home and cooks, cleans, and looks after the kids?" Donna replies, "How about mule?"

In Freud's *Jokes and Their Relation to the Unconscious* (1960), he suggests that there is truth in humor, particularly in tendentious jokes that release some form of aggression or hostility that is otherwise repressed. He writes that "The prevention of invective or insulting rejoinders by external circumstances is such a common case that tendentious jokes are particularly favored in order to make aggression or critique possible against persons in exalted positions who can exercise authority. The joke then represents a rebellion against that authority, liberation from its pressure" (125).

Here Donna expresses her resentment at the fact that she is basically a worker in the home, economically dependent on Alex and tied to the social mores that render her subservient to men. Her joke demonstrates her need to defy authority and to relieve the emotions that are typically repressed as she performs her domestic duties. Humor here becomes a substitute for anger, much as Mellencamp (2003) describes the use of humor by Gracie Allen and Lucille Ball in their respective programs. There is a surreal moment that defuses the tension, though, as Donna's vacuum cleaner then begins to repeat the word "housewife." Donna's thoughts are displaced onto the object that is made to appear animate, and for a moment suburbia is made to seem unreal. She flicks the switch on and off, but the sound continues. There is laughter on the sound track, and attention is deflected from the tendentious joke to a comic moment that is absurd rather than hostile.

There are other ways in which *The Donna Reed Show* contests the traditional housewife role that women adopted in television sitcoms of the time, first and foremost because the show revolves around Donna Stone's point of view. While June Cleaver and Margaret Anderson were often superfluous and we rarely learned about what their days were like, in the majority of episodes Donna Stone occupies center frame, is shot in close-up, and, until later seasons when Donna Reed was tired because of her difficult work schedule, is almost always the subject of the story line. Carl Betz acknowledged his secondary position: "Donna and Tony are friends of mine. . . . But I never kidded myself about the series. Basically, they wrote for Donna. I had maybe three episodes that were good for me" (Royce 1990, 8). While both *Leave It to Beaver* and *Father Knows Best* focus on the importance of the father in the family unit, *The Donna Reed Show* makes the housewife the central figure.

Like June Cleaver and Margaret Anderson, Donna Stone ultimately subordinates her needs to those of her family. Unlike June Cleaver or Margaret Anderson, Donna Stone is highly visible and vocal and propels much of the action. In an era when men dominated sitcoms, Donna Reed not only was the star of her own show but was also the axial character within the narrative; she took center stage while the other characters, including her television husband played by Carl Betz, remained subordinate in terms of both screen space and story line. In terms of the narrative, Donna Reed/Stone is clearly in charge: she behaves independently and manipulates situations and characters to her advantage. Donna Stone often puts her own needs first. In "A Very Merry Christmas," for example, Donna is tired of the consumerism that surrounds Christmas and decides to spend Christmas Eve with the sick children at the hospital. Buster Keaton guest stars as the hospital janitor whom she enlists to play Santa Claus, and together they provide gifts for children in need. But Donna's good deed means that in order for her family to spend Christmas Eve together, the Stones have to join her in the hospital where she brings cheer to other people's children. When Donna decides to become a writer in "Author, Author," she neglects her family. She begins and ends the series as a character whose behavior is often not dependent on her husband or children, despite the social expectations for women in the late 1950s and early 1960s.

"The Beaded Bag" is rife with references to how women manipulate men to get "surprised" by gifts that they have already selected. Donna observes a masterful saleswoman selling such a piece of jewelry to a man. "It was merciful," the saleswoman observes. "He never knew what hit him." Donna eyes an expensive bag that she wants for her birthday and decides that it is just too much money, but after a plot twist or two she manages to get it in the end. In "The First Time We Met," Donna gives her friend advice on how to land a husband by telling her to appear uninterested and to refuse him when he asks for dates. "Men are like fish. They all wind up getting caught if you use the right bait," Donna tells her. It becomes apparent later in the episode that Donna manipulated her first meeting with Alex to make it appear coincidental. While these episodes may not be an entirely flattering representation of feminine wiles, they also portray a strong female who can outsmart the unwitting men (and women) around her.

Donna Stone is active in the community and is often outside the domestic sphere: she performs as an amateur actress,

Buster Keaton appears in "A Very Merry Christmas." (Courtesy of The Donna Reed Foundation)

volunteers at the hospital, heads fund-raising and charitable organizations, is a member of the PTO, and participates in a women's club. She is political and is not shy about entering the typically male public sphere: she gives speeches, runs for town council, and tries to fight city hall when she feels she has a case. In "Tony Martin Visits," for example, an episode that guest starred the then-popular singer in a cameo role, Donna gets a parking ticket and goes to court to fight it, despite the fact that this means that her family vacation will have to be postponed. Once again she puts her needs in front of the family's, and they are dismayed that their long-awaited vacation is put on hold so that she can prove a point. When Donna goes to court to arrange a hearing, she meets Tony Martin, who is protesting a speeding ticket he received as he passed through town. Her spunk convinces the singing star to further delay his own trip to argue his case in court. In the end he wins, but Donna is proven wrong. The show falls just short of championing the assertive woman: while she is claiming that she didn't deserve a ticket because she was parked legally, in fact she miscalculated the time left on her meter. Her entire complaint has been a case of misguided logic, and so she is cast as silly rather than strong. Yet again, however, throughout the episode we have seen her put her own needs ahead of her family's as she tries to fight city hall.

Donna Stone's life does not revolve around the family. She has any number of female friends, and her neighbor Midge is a regular on the show. Friends frequently call and drop by, and the Stones have a vibrant social life, with a steady stream of dinner parties and social engagements. When they have company, they even serve cocktails! Donna and Alex are often mysteriously out for the evening when the children become involved in various mishaps. In "Boys Will Be Boys," Donna and Alex disappear for the evening even though their houseguest is a troubled boy on weekend leave from military school. In "A Night to Howl," they decide to shake up their routine by going out on the town midweek. In "Decisions, Decisions," they appear at a nightclub to go dancing after Mary and her date have called it a night, and Donna and Alex seem to be on a first-name basis with the staff.

"Rebel with a Cause" is an interesting comment on consumer culture and the targeting of housewives by market research that simultaneously displays Donna Stone's independent streak. A marketing firm selects Donna for a research project because she and twenty-four other women in Hilldale fit the profile of "TAW": the average woman. She is initially flattered when the marketing company representative visits and provides her with a device to measure how much time she spends doing chores during the week. He stays for dinner, and she overhears him bragging to the family that he could predict that they would have leftovers and chocolate cake for dessert because that's what "average" housewives serve at the end of the week. Donna becomes insulted and resents the claim that her behavior is predictable. The following day, the Hilldale newspaper editor asks her to help him with a story about a reclusive real estate tycoon who was a friend of her family's, and she relishes the chance to prove that she is not an average housewife. The rest of the episode becomes slapstick comedy as she sneaks into the hotel where the family friend is staying, dons a maid's costume, adopts an Irish accent, and engages in high jinks as the hotel manager chases her through the hallways. In the end, she finds the family friend and gets the story, which, to the astonishment of her family, is published in the town newspaper. Both the stylistic departure and the content of the episode demonstrate that Donna Stone is not TAW.

We often see the tension between Donna Stone's feminine masquerade and her desire to break free of her socially restricted role. *The Donna Reed Show* spanned the period from the postwar domestic containment of women to the women's liberation movement of the 1960s, and in many ways the show speaks to the women's movement that came to fruition during the period of the show's run. The episode "Trees," made in 1966, seems to argue for the efficacy of civil disobedience and of social activism in support of a principle in which one believes. The episode does not directly address the women's movement or the antiwar movement, but the unusual form departs from the realism that is characteristic of the series and in so doing works on the level of allegory. As the episode begins, Donna is upset because the city is going to cut down her carob tree and replace it with a tidier elm tree that will fit in with the other trees in the neighborhood. The city official tells her that she needs to register a complaint with Commissioner Trimmit. Rather than playing his standard character, Jeff seems to serve here as representative of the social order; he robotically quotes from a municipal law book and tells Donna that the city has a

right to cut down the tree. The men in this episode are nota-
bly passive. First Alex and later Dave Kelsey simply tell their
wives that you can't fight city hall. Donna responds, "That may
be true. But when they come over here to try to cut down my
carob tree, they are fighting *me*." The next scene documents the
frustrations of the citizen who does try to fight city hall and
is mired in bureaucratic red tape that exists for no apparent
reason. When she goes Commissioner Trimmit's office to put in
an official complaint, he turns out to be the same city official
who had been at her house the day before. The commissioner's
secretary tells her that she needs a pass and that no exceptions
are ever granted. To get the pass, she needs to fill out a lengthy
form that is referred to as a "time-saving device," a term evoca-
tive of Orwellian doublespeak. Similarly, the conversation that
Donna has with the administrator in charge of the second form
exemplifies the use of language that fails to communicate in
bureaucratic culture. Donna hands the form to the secretary,
who makes a phone call and says, "We have a serious problem on our hands." Donna, thinking that the woman is sym-
pathetic, answers, "It certainly is. They're going to cut it down
first thing in the morning." However, the problem is that it is
unclear which form Donna should be filling out, whether it's
tree cutting or tree trimming. To be safe, the woman insists that
Donna fill out a duplicate form. Donna arrives back in Commissioner Trimmit's office with her arms full of papers. When
the secretary asks Donna what they are, she cynically answers,
"Time-saving devices."

When Donna finally gains an audience with Commissioner
Trimmit, he threatens to not hear her complaint because she
failed to put in her grandmother's birthplace, another reference
to the overbureaucratization of government. The commissioner
agrees to hear Donna's complaint when she threatens to speak
to the mayor, and his words belie everything that has happened
before in the episode when he tells her, "I'm no petty bureau-
crat. I'm no stickler for red tape." He stamps her form and says,

"There you are, all processed. You just wind up and toss that complaint pitch right across home plate." Donna pleads her case for the authentic, original carob tree, but the commissioner is unmoved. He tells her that he is going to replace her carob tree with a brand new elm because that's "progress." When she protests that she doesn't want a new tree, he introduces the theme of conformity: "Today you don't, but tomorrow you will, because everyone else has one." After Donna leaves, he opens his mouth and growls, with the sound track exaggerating the sound, a comedic device that is repeated throughout the episode.

The critique here is of a culture that values the new over the old and modernity over tradition and where originality has been replaced by conformity. This is a comment on middle-class suburbia and the idealized images of social conformity that were increasingly under attack by the more liberal culture of the mid-1960s. As with the women's liberation movement, it is the women of suburbia who organize to protest social injustice. Donna holds the equivalent of a consciousness-raising group in her living room. She addresses her female neighbors assembled before her: "Are we going to be passive victims to regimentation? Slaves to conformity? Thank you women of Elm Street. And remember, united we stand."

After each question, the women respond "No" in unison and finally clap when Donna has finished speaking. They unite to protest Commissioner Trimmit's decision. In step, they march into his office wearing identical suits, hats, and purses. They hold scripts from which they chant "This is the world of the future. We are the women of Elm Street. We dress alike and talk alike and think alike and we are miserable. Who made us this way?" They point to the commissioner: "You. Is this what you want? We don't want uniformity. Do you want *us* to be like *this*?"

While they are ostensibly discussing trees, their comments could be referring to any number of ways in which women were

The women of Elm Street join together to protest conformity in "Trees."

encouraged to conform at the time, and the image suggests that
women united could take control of their lives. The commissioner aptly refers to their visit as a "demonstration" that was
staged to intimidate him, and he vows to defeat the protestors.
The conflict escalates as he refers to the incident as "Operation Uniformity" and draws up a battle plan. But when he arrives the next day to take down the carob tree, he finds Donna
sitting in it, reading a fashion magazine. She claims that the
tree is her home and refuses to get down. The women of Elm
Street, who had been hiding behind the bushes, jump up in
unison and shout "Yes!" Jeff then emerges from the house with
the municipal law book that says that the commissioner will
need an eviction notice and must give ninety days' warning.
Donna is demonstrating peaceful nonresistance and using the
law to fight the law. Whereas the men on the show are resigned
and argue that you can't fight the system, Donna does just that.

The episode ends with a reference to the power of media. Just as the exasperated commissioner climbs up the tree to confront Donna, a news truck arrives. Afraid of bad publicity, he backs down and says that he has reversed his decision on "Operation Uniformity."

"Trees," made in 1966, is far removed from the 1950s' domestic family sitcom in which women were invisible and subordinate to their husbands and had no voice in public affairs. "Trees" was a stylistically unusual episode that departed from the melodramatic realism that marked most episodes of the show, displaying more in common with absurdist theater that exposed the illogical experiences at the heart of everyday life. This was as close as *The Donna Reed Show* came to addressing the social and political turmoil that marked the country in the 1960s and to critiquing the conformism that marked the culture of the 1950s. "Trees" advocated the necessity of social protest and the right to demonstrate to support one's beliefs, and its resolution suggested that women working in unison could overturn "the system." It was probably no coincidence that the episode aired during the program's final season, when Donna Reed was ready to stop playing Donna Stone, the ideal wife and mother, and was about to become more active in public life. In a 2008 interview, Paul Petersen addressed the question of whether *The Donna Reed Show* was a feminist milestone or millstone:

> Well look, people were extraordinarily careful in the construction and production of "The Donna Reed Show," not only to the sensitivities of the audience but also as to the characters we portrayed. That stemmed from their early experience into the power of the medium. So we were trying to do something positive, and it always amazed us, especially as the years went on, that people who didn't watch the show sort of took their cue from Johnny Carson, who was really not very kind to Donna. And even

though it was a source of some amusement, there's only one other woman that owns her own show in television, and that's Lucille Ball. Television in those days, our agenda was straightforward. We were there to sell Campbell's Soup, not to change hearts and minds. (Plath 2008)

As Petersen points out (perhaps confusing Johnny Carson with Jack Parr and David Susskind, who were known to joke about the show's wholesome image), the image of Donna Reed/Donna Stone remains that of the perfect housewife and mom, particularly among people who only vaguely remember the show or those who didn't watch it in the first place. Fultz (1998, 133) observes that the level of criticism that the show drew came from the fact that "for the first time on weekly television, a pretty, soft-spoken, intelligent, youngish suburban Mommy was actually the lead." For many viewers, the show seemingly aligned itself with patriarchal postwar culture, although the tensions and contradictions inherent in this ideology could not help but be expressed in a program that was all about the mother. While limited by the formula of the domestic sitcom, Donna Stone showed women how to engage in the world, outside of the confines of the domestic sphere. She showed women that femininity was a masquerade and that it could be performed in any number of ways.

Teen Culture and *The Donna Reed Show*

*T*he *Donna Reed Show* was somewhat unusual in that the Stone children, Mary and Jeff, were already teenagers when the show went on the air in 1958. This was a strategic choice, since Donna Reed had a one-year-old daughter at the time that the show began. She explained in an interview that "There are plenty of women my age who look no older than I do and they have teenage children. In Hollywood it just wasn't done. So we did it!" ("The Farmer's Daughter Who Went to Town" 1961, 13). At the start of the eight-year series, Jeff was fourteen and Mary sixteen, and so the show took place in the context of the postwar phenomenon of the baby boom generation and the development of teen culture. Although many writers suggest that the teenager as a social category is a post–World War II phenomenon, teen culture developed as early as the 1920s through "the celebration of youth, the evolution of commercial leisure and consumer culture, and the steady rise in high school enrollment" (Schrum 2004, 15). However, the importance of the teen became heightened in the postwar period as the baby boomers born in the late 1940s and early 1950s began to reach adolescence and marketers became aware of the buying power of the teen demographic. By the early 1960s, millions of young

Americans were entering puberty. According to Douglas (1994, 61), the growth rate of this population took off at four times the average of all the other age groups, and forty-six million Americans entered their teens in this decade.

Jeff and Mary Stone were the classic baby boomers. They entered puberty in the late 1950s and early 1960s, and like *The Donna Reed Show* itself, they were representative of the transition from the conservative 1950s to the more liberal 1960s. *The Donna Reed Show* negotiated the cultural shift toward more permissive parenting that was part of larger debates around the national character in the wake of World War II. According to Spigel (2001, 224–25), in both intellectual and popular culture, critics worried that an autocratic style of parenting, as opposed to one that was nurturing and egalitarian, would develop the kinds of personalities that were unsuited for the basic goals of the free world. Child-rearing experts such as Dr. Benjamin Spock, who advocated a liberal and permissive approach to parenting, articulated the cultural discourse around parenting that circulated in the culture. Jenkins (n.d.) writes that "By the 1950s, permissiveness, although not without its detractors, had become the dominant discourse about childhood within postwar American society, promoted by a seemingly endless flood of childcare books, prescriptive articles in women's magazines, and advertisements; its implications were explored by learned sociologists, psychologists and anthropologists but also pervaded popular culture, shaping the comic books, television, films, records, and children's books of the period."

In many ways, *The Donna Reed Show* is a primer on the boundaries and tensions of permissive parenting. The show negotiates the new terrain of a generation in which children were often indulged and had more free time and money than in the past and in which a more democratic style—with all of its advantages and disadvantages—had replaced the more autocratic tenets of previous generations. Donna Reed's position on permissive parenting was mirrored in Donna Stone (or vice versa).

Donna Reed gave parenting advice in popular magazines that illuminated the permissively directive style of her character. In "Donna Reed: She Puts The Family First," she advocates giving children allowances but only for doing chores and also advocates helping them with their problems without being obtrusive about it (Lewis 1964, 44). Her behavior with the child actors on the set is described similarly: "Without showing any muscle, Donna has quietly worked to shape Paul's tastes and attitudes" (Anderson 1965). The feminism that was later attributed to Donna Reed also comes through in her stated belief that young girls work before marriage "to get away from the idea of becoming wife and mother and nothing else" (Lewis 1964, 43). Overall, just like in the television show, Donna Reed promoted the importance of a strong family unit: "We're living in a codeless era, and all I say is that a young person should live by some code—and a code set by one's parents is best" (Gregory 1964).

Despite Donna Reed's advice on parenting, parents had less influence on their children than in the past. As more children were encouraged to make decisions for themselves and as more finished high school and attended college, peer groups grew in importance, leading to the societal tensions that marked what became known as the generation gap. *The Donna Reed Show* gently touches upon the tensions that emerged in the 1960s when the choices made by teenagers were sometimes in conflict with their parents, although its narrative resolutions always place Donna Stone as simultaneously firm and lenient, wise and understanding. She knows what's best for her children and will do whatever it takes to ensure that their choices accord with her wishes, though always with the caveat that they have freely chosen their behaviors.

Music was one way that teens defined themselves as separate from their parents, first with the advent of Elvis Presley in the 1950s and then the British Invasion that began with the arrival of the Beatles in the United States in the early 1960s. Apart from music, the media also exacerbated fears of this newly empowered generation by playing up fears of so-called juvenile delinquency, described in newspaper and magazine articles and explored in feature films such as *Rebel Without a Cause, Blackboard Jungle,* and *Splendor in the Grass.* In *The Donna Reed Show,* Mary and Jeff remain "good" kids, although the shadow of delinquency looms over them in plots in which they skirt with temptations to misbehave. In terms of teen sexuality, the birth control pill came on the market in 1960, which ushered in what came to be known as the Sexual Revolution. On *The Donna Reed Show,* appropriate behaviors regarding sex and dating were never part of the plotline even after Mary and then Jeff were in college, although occasional episodes express Donna's fear of Mary's emerging sexuality. Unlike films that explored more edgy material, television largely avoided complicated representations of teens, and both Mary and Jeff were examples of how well-socialized children learned to become just like their parents. The rambunctious Jeff had some elements of the so-called good bad boy, who according to Leslie Fiedler (1960, 270) is the quintessential American character who is crude and unruly but ultimately possesses an instinctive sense of what is right, seen in youthful male characters such as Dennis the Menace. Mary Stone, on the other hand, was a younger version of Donna Stone, who showed few signs of teenage rebellion or rejection of her parents' values. In many episodes, Mary is positioned in a two-shot alongside Donna, often in opposition to Alex and Jeff, in order to emphasize their similarity.

As teens increasingly mobilized and rebelled against their parents in the culture and in cinematic representations of youths, Mary and Jeff Stone remained well disciplined and under control, kept in line by Donna's guiding hand and common sense. *The Donna Reed Show* operated within the generic constraints of a conventional sitcom in which problems were trivial and contained within the episode, and its representations of teenage life were no exception. In a period marked by the Cold War, the assassination of President John F. Kennedy, the Vietnam War, the women's and civil rights movements, and the rise of the counterculture, the teenagers on *The Donna Reed Show* largely remained ensconced in dances, dating, and college life (without the demonstrations). However, social anxieties were not entirely absent.

Despite *The Donna Reed Show*'s attempt to avoid controversy and to maintain the image of the idealized nuclear family, there were episodes in which the show addressed the trepidation around teen behavior that characterized the social milieu. As is characteristic of melodrama, anxieties seeped out, only to be ultimately contained within the narrative of the show. *The Donna Reed Show* marked its cultural moment through episodes about music, drugs, teenage rebellion, and dating.

Music

While television in its infancy assumed a cohesive domestic unit gathered around the set, by the late 1950s it became apparent that television could appeal to the burgeoning teen demographic through popular music. While we speak today of synergy and cross-promotion, *The Donna Reed Show* similarly used television as a platform to promote musical stars under contract to Columbia's recording arm, Colpix Records. *The Donna Reed Show* showcased musical guests James Darren, Tony Martin, and Lesley Gore, all of whom sang their songs on the show. Both Darren and Gore were teen idols at the time they made their appearances, while Martin appealed to a somewhat older demographic. Not coincidentally, these were pop rather than rock and roll singers who sang soft harmonious songs of love and romance rather than more edgy (and threatening to adults) rock and roll music. Darren appeared on the series in a first-season episode, "April Fool," as a way to promote both his music and the soon-to-be released film *Gidget,* in which he starred. He plays popular singer Buzz Berry, who comes to Hilldale to play a concert date. The episode comments on the generational rift in musical tastes and listening habits, with Donna criticizing Mary for listening to his record eleven times and Alex referring to it as "horrible music." The generational divide is further established when Mary announces in exaggerated fashion that she will "just die" if she doesn't get tickets to his concert, and Alex queries, "What is it about the guitar-playing crooner that turns teenage girls into wild animals?" The record is "There's No Such Thing as the Next Best Thing to Love," Darren's first Colpix single that he would also sing in *Gidget*.

When Buzz Berry catches the measles and has to cancel the concert, Alex is of course the doctor, and the singing star ends up hiding from his fans at the Stones' house. When Mary tells her friends and they refuse to believe her, one snidely remarks, "We were expecting Elvis but the army couldn't spare him."

While Elvis Presley and the subsequent British Invasion had a significant impact on teenage culture during the run of *The Donna Reed Show* and the show itself capitalized on the burgeoning teen audience for popular music, apart from this one reference to Elvis, the more "troubling" elements of popular music were ignored. It is not accidental that the character Buzz Berry, whose music is so foreign to Alex and Donna Stone, is clean-cut, self-effacing, and the model of propriety. When Darren returns again in season 4, he plays yet another singing star, this time named Jim Brandt, who is hiding his identity and pretending to be an ordinary person named Kip Dennis whom Mary dates, yet another unthreatening representation of the rock and roll star.

In 1966 Gore, then one of the most popular vocalists in the United States, appeared as herself in the final episode of the series to air. She was one of the first protofeminist singers to emerge in the early 1960s, known for songs such as "It's My Party" and "You Don't Own Me," the latter of which addressed female independence rather than longing for love. In "Jeff's By-Line," she visits Hilldale and sings "We Know We're in Love," a song from her then-current album rather than one of her more assertive female-centered songs. In the episode's story line, the song is penned by Jeff and his friend Scotty, who are honored to have Gore perform it on stage, and she then tells them that she is going to record it (and of course, she already has). In this way, the show is cross-promoting stars under contract to Colpix and giving them an opportunity to perform their music in front of millions of television viewers. Again, any subversive messages that can be attributed to popular music are tamed, even in a singer known for challenging the limited range of topics available to female musicians.

More crucially, the show developed singing careers for its own teenage stars, Shelley Fabares and Paul Petersen. ABC used sitcoms to appeal to teen viewers early on, beginning when Ricky Nelson sang a version of Fats Domino's "I'm Walkin'" on *The Adventures of Ozzie and Harriet* in 1957 and later when Johnny Crawford from *The Rifleman* had his first hit single in 1962. The idea for launching singing careers for Fabares and Petersen is attributed to Tony Owen, who decided after the second season that songs would be written into the scripts and arranged for Colpix Records to release them. *The Donna Reed Show*'s theme song composer Stu Phillips worked with the two actors, despite the fact that neither could sing. According to Fabares, "Both Paul and I said it was a great idea, but I couldn't sing. I was adamant. I'm not a singer" (Bronson 2003, 107).

According to Fultz (1998, 145), when Fabares sent Phillips her demo tape, he responded, "Oh well. We can make anyone sound like anything." Fabares recorded "Johnny Angel" in an echo chamber to enhance her voice, repeating the lyrics twice and dubbing them over one another in a process called double tracking to make her voice sound stronger. Experienced studio musicians Glen Campbell and Hal Blaine and backup singers Darlene Love and The Blossoms also helped produce the song. The result, "Johnny Angel," was written into season 4's "Donna's Prima Donna." In the episode, Mary decides that she is going to try for a singing career rather than go to college. Donna convinces Mary to visit the college campus anyway, where she is promised a singing gig at the end of the day. Throughout the episode, Donna uses reverse psychology to convince Mary to make her own decision that will favor what Donna wants, which is for Mary to opt for the security of a college education over the vicissitudes of a singing career. But Donna is stunned at the episode's end when Mary sings her song. She is convinced that Mary has talent, although Mary, swayed and manipulated by her mother, decides to attend college after all. Ironically, the song did spur Fabares to leave *The Donna Reed Show* to pursue a singing and acting career. "Johnny Angel" went to number one on the Billboard charts and sold more than a million copies. Unlike the early work of Gore that speaks to female independence, "Johnny Angel" is a love song in which she laments that "Johnny" doesn't even know she exists. She turns down dates with other boys so that she can be near the phone if he calls. The song was a hit despite its rather nonsensical premise: how can he call her if he doesn't know she exists?

Fabares and Petersen collaborated on several songs and record albums. Individual songs such as "She Can't Find Her Keys" (sung by Fabares and Petersen) aired on the show. Petersen's solo effort, "My Dad," was his only single that made it to the Billboard top ten. There was an attempt made to place the songs organically within the context of the show: Mary was purportedly a singer in the school band, and Jeff, like many teenage boys, formed his own band that practiced in the garage. In the episode "My Dad," which aired in 1962, Jeff is upset because Alex keeps missing family events because of his busy work schedule. Alex arrives too late to hear Jeff perform the song, but the band convinces him to play it again backstage. As he sings, the camera closes in on Alex, who listens apart from Donna and Mary. He stands backstage, and high-contrast theatrical lighting emphasizes his reaction as he wipes away tears, as do Donna and Mary in their own two-shot.

As Fabares's singing career began to develop, there was less

Mary sings "Johnny Angel" in "Donna's Prima Donna."

of an effort made to weave her songs into the show's narrative. In season 5's "Big Star" (her last season, when she made occasional appearances on the show), she tries to convince her music professor that her boyfriend has singing talent. She succeeds, he performs a song, and the professor recognizes that he is gifted. At the conclusion of the episode, Mary sings "Big Star" as she laments that he will now move on. But this appears more as an extradiegetic commentary on the episode than a part of the narrative. It is a way to release another single, and there is no pretense of it playing a part in the diegetic story.

Both Fabares and Petersen also went on to make three record albums with Darren during 1962–63, all produced by Phillips and on the Colpix record label: music from the film *Bye Bye Birdie* along with the albums *Teenage Triangle* and *More Teenage Triangle*. In this context, it is amusing to look back at scenes from 1959's "April Fool," in which Mary almost faints when she is introduced to Buzz and Jeff lip-synchs the words to Buzz's songs. While Petersen may have recognized his limitations as a singer and did not pursue a musical career, Fabares began to believe in the image of the teenage pop star that had been constructed for her. Although she had some later success in film and television, her musical career did not prosper in the wake of "Johnny Angel."

Teenage Rebellion

In *Living Room Lectures,* Leibman (1995) distinguishes between film and television with regard to the way they dealt with socially inappropriate and delinquent behavior. Juvenile delinquency was a major social concern in the 1950s and early 1960s, perceptions of which were exacerbated by the media. But in contrast to film, television programs, outside of the police procedural, did not typically delve into social dilemmas such as divorce, abandonment, teen rebellion, and juvenile delinquency. Liebman writes:

> In a two-pronged strategy designed to underscore the consumptive imperatives of commercial television, the programs first recognize the untoward activity and then appropriate it into mainstream culture and the province of parental authority. By assuming the mantle of authority, the parents in the television family confiscate the very rebellions of youth. While there are many examples of this strategy, it is put to its most potent use in episodes dealing with rock and roll and juvenile delinquency (manifest by fighting and joyriding). (1995, 354)

Most, though not all, episodes of *The Donna Reed Show* conform to Leibman's (1995) characterization. She cites an early episode, "Pardon My Gloves," as an example of the sanctioning of fighting as a way to assert masculinity. When Jeff is repeatedly beat up on the way home from school, Donna and then Alex teach him how to box. Both parents support the idea of Jeff using physical violence to attack the offending boy, and such behavior is acceptable so long as it is within the context of parental approval. In Leibman's words, they "appropriate fighting into the mainstream, defusing it, de-marginalizing it, and incorporating adult authority figures into its success" (56–57).

Parental anxieties always hover around the edges of the show. In seasons 1 and 2, the problematic youth is incorporated into *The Donna Reed Show* in the recurring character of David Barker, a troubled young boy who runs away from military school. In "Guest in the House," he spends Thanksgiving weekend with the Stone family. It quickly becomes apparent that all he needs is parental love, readily supplied by Donna. In the end, we learn that his overly strict father has left David in military school because he does not know how to care for the boy. David's father sees the error of his ways and promises to give the boy more attention, and thus proper parenting solves the family's problems, at least temporarily. When the now-tamer David returns for a visit in "Boys Will Be Boys," it is Jeff who instigates the naughty behavior. When Donna and Alex leave Jeff in charge for the evening, at Jeff's prompting the boys eat an entire chocolate cake and watch a gangster film that gives David a nightmare. Jeff has become the disobedient boy, although he is apologetic and remorseful at episode's end.

Jeff is portrayed as trouble prone but basically well adjusted. (Even so, Fultz [1998, 153] writes that the show was least popular in England because Jeff was considered a bad example for children.) There are no friends who play the bad boy in the mold of Eddie Haskell from *Leave It to Beaver;* if anything, Jeff has the characteristics of the good bad boy who is constantly causing trouble. He dominates the relationship with his best friend, Smitty, rather than the reverse, and Smitty often feels that Jeff is taking advantage of him. Jeff is always eating loudly;

in many episodes he chomps on an apple, often in the face of his sister Mary. Jeff and Mary argue frequently, although they are also shown to have a caring relationship. There is strong sibling rivalry, as in the episode "Jeff vs. Mary" when Jeff is convinced that his parents care more for his sister. Their quarrel in "Mary Comes Home," when Mary returns home from college to visit for the weekend, is quite harsh for a television sitcom.

But the show puts Jeff rather than Mary closer to the dangers associated with juvenile delinquency, even though he is always incorporated back into the family unit by learning his lesson. In "Jeff's Double Life," Mary gets reprimanded because her friends played the trumpet and bongo drums until 11:45 at night when Donna and Alex were out. (They were frequently not at home in late-season episodes.) A neighbor complains to Alex, telling him that she almost called the police. Mary assures her parents that it won't happen again, and Alex gives both Mary and Jeff a lecture about the need for a doctor's children to model good behavior. But in the same episode, Jeff actually does get involved with the police. He goes joyriding with a friend of Mary's who has taken his father's car without permission (in any other television show, this would be known as stealing), and the friend is driving without a license. When the police notice them, they engage in a car chase that ends with them crashing into a tree. While Jeff is innocent of any wrongdoing (he did not know that the friend had no license and was "borrowing" the car), he tries to keep his parents from learning about the incident, given Alex's earlier lecture. When Jeff ultimately confesses, all is forgiven. But the severity of the original transgression is never addressed, and Jeff is primarily admonished for not having open communication with his parents.

In season 2's "A Place to Go," Jeff and his friends, this time with Jeff instigating the mischief, break into an abandoned house to alleviate their boredom during summer vacation. The police find them and take them to the station but call their parents rather than arresting them. The fact that Jeff has forcibly pried a window open to enter the house does not come into play; instead, Donna decides that the problem is that the boys need a place to spend time. She organizes her women's club to fix up the abandoned house to make it into a clubhouse, only to realize that Jeff and his friends would rather spend a day exploring at the town dump than in a space determined by their parents. There is a slight reference to the existence of troubled youths when one of Donna's friend's comments, "Bad company, that's what leads them astray," only to learn that her own son was involved in the break-in. But for the most part, socially irresponsible behaviors are presented as merely mischievous, and the boys' desire to frequent spaces that are not circumscribed by parents is depicted as normal teen behavior. The clubhouse is abandoned, and the boys are left to their adventures in the dump.

The season 5 episode "Operation Anniversary" epitomizes the way that anxieties about male youths are introduced and then allayed. When Jeff is working late at night in the Kelseys' garage to make an anniversary present for his parents, Donna and Alex notice a shadowy figure that appears to be holding a gun silhouetted in the window. They only refrain from calling the police when the Kelseys eventually tell them that it is Jeff. Male threat is implied but mistaken, and Jeff is the good son who is of course working on a present for his parents rather than engaging in nefarious activity.

In the majority of episodes that center around Jeff, he is engaged in moneymaking schemes or dating mishaps, themes that keep him out of harm's way and normalize him as a typical teenage boy. Teenage rebellion, when it is addressed at all, is the province of acquaintances of the Stone family rather than Mary or Jeff. For the most part, real-life cultural disturbances brought about by social justice movements, the Vietnam War, and the counterculture did not exist in the world of Hilldale. Teenage rebellion was portrayed as a series of inconsequential mishaps or as the consequence of overly strict parenting. In season 8's

"Pop Goes Theresa," a girl named Theresa decides to disobey her overprotective father and arranges to meet Jeff for an afternoon date in the park. With her first taste of freedom, she takes off her shoes, begins to dance and whoop like an Indian, and runs into the woods and picks all the flowers (to Jeff's somewhat puzzled consternation). Jeff offers to take her to Murphy's Pizza, where she has presumably never been, and she shouts, "This is going to be the grandest afternoon of my life. Yippee!" When they get to Murphy's, she compares her plight with that of East Europeans: "I've broken through the iron curtain. I'm liberated! I'm free! I got out!" In response one boy starts playing the guitar, and the entire group of Jeff's friends starts clapping and singing, "She got out! She got out!" They march in and out of the kitchen and begin dancing on the tables, while Mr. Murphy keeps telling them to quiet down. The teens are out of control but in an orderly way, marching in rhythm and to the tune of the guitar.

The police arrive and take the dancing teens to the station, where the police officer informs his sergeant that "They were dancing on the tabletops, breaking up plates, and—swimming in the kitchen." His reference allows a riff on the generation gap and the then new dance that was called the Swim. The sergeant is confused, and Jeff politely tells him, "You don't understand, sir. Swimming is dancing." Theresa interjects, "I'll show you." She begins to do the Swim again and starts another round of teens singing and dancing to the tune of "She got out." Two of the dancing teens are black, which is the first and only indication that Jeff's social circle in Hilldale is integrated. Both Theresa's father and Donna arrive, at which point the term "juvenile delinquent" is used. He informs Donna, "Your son is a delinquent and I'm going to see him put behind bars as sure as my name is Brad Marshall." Upon recognizing his name as that of a college classmate, Donna tells the sergeant, "He was the worst juvenile delinquent there was—when there weren't any." She describes his rather tame college high jinks—crashing the girl's sorority—as an example of his "delinquent" behavior. The label "juvenile delinquent" is invoked, but the definition seems to be more that of prankster than social menace. Donna then talks to Theresa's father and convinces him that he has restricted her too much, sanctioning a more permissive, democratic, Dr. Spock style of parenting. Theresa is rebellious but in the most innocent way possible and only because of her father's unreasonable demands. Her rebelliousness is nothing that Donna's wise parenting won't cure.

There is one season 8 episode, however, that is issue-oriented and socially relevant and in which problems are not resolved within the family unit. Visually, it is an unusual episode with chiascuro lighting and only a sparse muted laugh track. "The Big League Shock" deals with a college friend of Jeff's, Bill Dayton, who had been class valedictorian in his small-town high school but who was getting average grades in college. He responds by studying harder but fails to do better and is clearly becoming emotionally unbalanced. Bill visits the Stones to use their encyclopedias, and when Jeff asks him where he's been lately, he closes Jeff down by shouting through clenched teeth, "I'm having enough trouble concentrating!" Bill falls asleep studying and at 5:00 a.m. wakes up screaming from a nightmare. Alex and Donna come downstairs to see that he is all right, and when he is alone with Alex, Bill asks for a pep pill to keep awake. Alex responds with a sermon to warn against the dangers of drug abuse. Shot in close-up, the scene becomes a public service announcement as he tells Bill, "You know these pills get you into a vicious cycle. First pep pills to keep you awake. Then you get too charged up to sleep so you need a pill to knock you out. Then before you've slept that off you need another pill to get you awake again." Needless to say, he refuses to give Bill the pills.

As Bill prepares to leave, he begins fiddling with Alex's medical bag. When Donna enters the room, Bill tells her he was just admiring it, but after he leaves Donna confides in Alex that

Jeff's friend Bill is jailed for stealing a drug prescription from Alex in "The Big League Shock."

she thinks he may have taken something. Coincidentally, later in the day Donna is at the pharmacist's where Bill is waiting to have his prescription filled. After he leaves, the pharmacist complains to Donna that Alex's handwriting on the prescription is illegible. She takes the prescription back to Alex, who confirms that it was stolen. He is about to call the police when the police call them and say that Bill has turned himself in. The Stones go to see him in jail, where he is filmed in close-up behind bars in a shadowy jail cell. He is deeply disturbed; he screams when Donna tries to reason with him and at first is angry rather than repentant. For the first time, Donna cannot say anything to remedy the situation. "Going to jail is bad, but being expelled from school is worse" are her rather inadequate words of wisdom. A problem of this magnitude can only be handled outside the home by authorities who specialize in these matters. While in early seasons of *The Donna Reed Show* psychology was often invoked only to show that Donna's good sense could outmatch the experts, here Donna is out of her element. Alex arrives with the college psychiatrist who offers to help Bill and says that he can stay in school. They are shot from a low angle, behind the jail cell bars, with deep shadows etched on both of their faces as Bill spits back, "That's ridiculous. Why don't you all mind your own business? I'm in jail and I should stay in jail." The psychiatrist matches Bill's tirade with harsh tough love that forces Bill to face himself: "So you can run home? A victim of poor judgment instead of poor grades?" Donna and Alex exchange a glance of admiration as he continues: "Bill, how are you going to face yourself? You haven't failed unless you quit. So give yourself a chance."

While Donna can solve the everyday problems of her family and friends, when it comes to a serious issue such as drug abuse, professionals are required. The resolution is quite unusual and indicates that *The Donna Reed Show*, at this juncture, is aligning itself with a larger cultural shift to relying on experts to solve problems that had once been in the domain of the family. Psychology was a relatively new science, and as historian George Lipsitz (1986, 91–92) points out, the reliance on child-rearing experts such as psychologists was a function of the decline of traditional sources of authority—both the father and the extended family—that emerged in the postwar cultural milieu. While in other episodes psychology is often invoked only to show that the new science is no match for Donna, here there is a shift to sources of authority outside of the family. Overall, the episode is far more dramatic than comedic or even melodramatic. Pep pills, stealing prescriptions from doctors, and jail cells are not typical fare for the domestic sitcom. Bill is clearly a disturbed mentally ill young man, and his anger and pain are quite discomfiting, which drove home the antidrug message. The episode later won a civic award for providing drug education. Yet Bill uses drugs to study rather than recreationally, and so the show still avoids the 1960s' drug culture even while engaging with it.

Dating

Parental anxieties around dating and teen sexuality tended to focus on Mary more so than Jeff. While Jeff dates and has many girlfriends, there is very little to indicate that Donna and Alex question his behavior. In season 8, they are concerned when they think that he wants to marry his girlfriend Bebe, but sex is not the issue. Yet in season 3's "Do You Trust Your Child?" they are terrified when Mary goes on a date with a boy who advocates "juvenarchy" because matriarchy and patriarchy have failed, and their faces pale when he tells Mary in coded language that fourteen-year-olds in other countries "take on adult responsibilities." Throughout the series, despite the fact that it includes teenage children, sexuality is primarily connected to Donna and Alex, and just as Donna fails to be contained domestically throughout the series, her sexuality slips through on occasion. While Donna and Alex sleep in twin beds, they clearly have a romantic and physical relationship. Alex often visits Donna in her bed, and they are shot in a tight close-up when he leans over to talk with her, so that they appear to be together. Their kisses are frequently long and passionate. In some episodes, there are clearly innuendos. For example, at the end of "The Male Ego," they have recovered from a quarrel and are going to bed. Donna asks Alex if he wants a glass of hot milk. He pulls her back into the bedroom, embraces her, and replies, "Man does not live by hot milk alone," and we hear the sentimental "Happy Days" theme music as the closing credits roll. In "The Fatal Leap," Donna frets that Alex is misbehaving at his college roommate's bachelor party. When Alex arrives home, Donna learns that he has had a boring evening and surmises, "I guess it's all right for girls to be with girls once in a while and for men to be with men." He leans over her in her twin bed, and again they are shot in extreme close-up. "The most fun is girls AND boys, isn't it?" he asks her. She agrees, and they have a long romantic kiss in bed as the screen fades to black.

There are no such romantic moments in Jeff and Mary's lives. The show provided a manual on the postwar phenomenon of dating and going steady, but, as Wini Breines (1992, 125) notes in *Young, White, and Miserable,* there was never any negotiation of sex, "making out," or even petting on television programs featuring teen life and behavior. Mary is presented as popular with boys, and many episodes are preoccupied with her deciding between two boys or finding the appropriate date for a dance. Although we see Mary and Jeff at home doing new dances that require them to move and shake to their own rhythms, at high school and college events they still dress in suits and dresses and dance formally in couples. Mary has a semisteady boyfriend, Scotty, although he is clearly the proverbial boy next door who teaches her to drive but does not kindle romantic passion. In most episodes, Mary takes Donna's advice on how to use her feminine wiles to win over some boy, and Donna seems to take pride in Mary's ability to manipulate the many boys who chase after her for dates. In "Mary's Double Date," for example, Alex is appalled that Mary is keeping two boys dangling about which she will take to the prom. He says to Mary, "If any girl ever did that to me I'd . . ." Donna interrupts him and says, "A girl did do that to you. You have two children with her." Even when Mary is in college before she leaves the show, there is far more emphasis on her social life than on her academics or career aspirations.

Mary is the "right kind of teen" who both looks and behaves like her mother. Season 5's "The New Look" (discussed in chapter 2) most clearly merges the two. The episode evokes the actress Donna Reed's desire to shake her wholesome image and play bad girls and, similarly, the actress Shelley Fabares's desire to break free of her role as Mary. Mary's desire to be bad emerges in a dream sequence in which she is alternately a flamboyant Southern belle and a smoldering nightclub dancer. But Mary is only a dangerous femme fatale in her dreams, and at the end of the episode she accepts that she is wholesome. Her character is proper and well behaved, despite the presence of potentially troublesome influences.

The early seasons also demonstrate parental anxieties around beatniks and beatnik culture. Breines (1992, 132) writes that "One of the peculiar characteristics of the 1950s, an expression of the powerful link between optimism and anxiety, was that fun-loving conformist teens existed side-by-side with disaffected teens—the delinquents, hoods, and Beatniks who loomed larger in the cultural and psychic life of America than their numbers might suggest."

There are no disaffected youth in Mary and Jeff's immediate social circles, although occasionally casual acquaintances remind viewers of the existence of a counterculture. In season 3's "Decisions, Decisions," Mary goes on a date with her boyfriend Roger and his "sophisticated" cousin to a club called the Hungry Onion. The club is small and dark and is sparsely populated, clearly a hangout for beatniks. As Mary waits for the pay phone so that she can call home, she hears a boy lying to his girlfriend about his whereabouts. He gives the phone to Mary and says, "Sorry I kept you waiting, like." Mary answers uneasily, "It's quite all right . . . Like." He then leans in and says, "You're a nice looking grasshopper. You ever fall up here before?" He is speaking a foreign language to Mary, who politely inquires, "I beg your pardon?" Later, on stage he recites a pretentious overwrought poem about man's futile attempt at immortality. Afterward he hovers over Mary's table and tells her that she inspired him to write it. When Roger asks him to explain it, jazzy music plays in the background as the boy replies in a stage whisper, "Daddio. It's like a butterfly's wings. When you explain it, you destroy it." Mary is uncomfortable rather than attracted to the atmosphere. Cultural otherness here is expressed through music, poetry, and beatnik language, and Mary wants no part of this. When Roger's cousin complains that Hilldale has no clubs like those in New York, Mary suggests that they go to the Flamingo, a more conventional nightclub that has an orchestra and a floor show. They spend the night there ordering dessert after dessert, but the boys don't have enough money to pay the bill. Mary, deeply embarrassed, leaves her special bracelet as collateral. Fortunately, after the teens leave, Donna and Alex happen to turn up for some late-night dancing. They are able to pay the bill and retrieve Mary's bracelet. Although Mary is out of her element in the expensive adult nightclub, she is clearly more at ease in the kind of place her parents frequent than in the beatnik Hungry Onion.

Despite Donna's claims to be in the camp of the permissive parent who trusts her children to make their own decisions (as she advocates in "Do You Trust Your Child?"), when it comes to dating, Donna does her best to maintain control. In "The Homecoming Dance," Mary's friend Herbie invites her to be his roommate's blind date at his college dance. Donna disapproves because Mary would have to stay in the dorms and asks Alex to have a talk with Mary. Alex, obeying Donna's request, awkwardly explains to Mary, "Boys go off to college and become men and that makes a difference. You know what I mean?" When she doesn't and insists on going, Donna and Alex decide that they will chaperone her (leaving the younger Jeff home alone for the weekend, but that does not worry them). When they arrive at the college, Donna's fears are confirmed when she overhears a boy-girl interaction:

> Boy: You're way out.
> Girl: I can see that you dig me.
> Boy: I have a sportscar.
> Girl: Man, that's the most.

The "danger" is coded by their use of beatnik lingo as a signifier of otherness. Donna is alarmed, and her fears are confirmed when the boy and girl leave together. Alex tells Donna to relax because "boys will be boys," and she replies, "That's what I'm worried about!" While sex is never mentioned, the prospect is clearly terrifying Donna. Not content with letting Mary handle her own affairs, they go to the dance to spy on her from the bushes outside. As in so many episodes of *The Donna Reed Show* and as is characteristic of melodrama, coincidence drives the plot. The boy whose conversation Donna has overheard earlier is indeed Mary's date, and they appear on the patio outside the dance exactly at the spot where Donna and Alex are crouched in the bushes. Donna witnesses the boy trying to kiss Mary and hears him using the same beatnik lines that she overheard earlier. But Mary is not that kind of girl and rebuffs the boy, which gives Donna a reprieve, at least temporarily, from her fears of teens, dating, and her daughter's sexuality.

Legacy of *The Donna Reed Show*

I have argued throughout this book that *The Donna Reed Show* is an important television milestone that exemplifies the cultural tensions that marked the shift from the conservative postwar Eisenhower era to the more liberal social context of the 1960s and 1970s, just as it marked a significant transitional moment as the film industry shifted to television. The sitcom, with its central place in American (and indeed global) television and its focus on familial and interpersonal relationships in the home or in the workplace, provides a site from which to explore how cultural meanings are made and from which to consider the relationship between television and culture. Domestic sitcoms such as *The Donna Reed Show* provide a glimpse into family life as it is conceived at a particular historical moment. They provide an often idealized behind-the-scenes look at gender and family relationships within a fictional community. In so doing, they are part of the communications apparatus that works to produce ideology; that is, they construct social reality and reproduce social relations. Lipsitz (1986, 107) writes that "Television, and other forms of electronic mass media, so effectively recapitulate the ideology of the 'historical bloc' in which they operate that they touch on all aspects of social life—even its antagonistic contradictions. While the media serve to displace, fragment, and atomize real experiences, they also generate and circulate a critical dialogue as one unintended consequence of their efforts to expose the inventory of social practice."

While in most cases television comedies attempt to smooth over contradictions, as we have seen with *The Donna Reed Show,* there is often trouble in the text that its melodramatic structure cannot contain. The show demonstrates Althusser's (2005, 255) principal of uneven development in social transformation: there are traces of older and progressive ways of thinking that coexist alongside dominant ideas and practices. In many ways, *The Donna Reed Show* remains within the confines of the conventional situation comedy and the ideology of domestic containment. Throughout the show's 275 episodes, the Stones' universe remains circumscribed: problems are slight and easily resolved, and there is little character development or transformation. The show in no way has the psychological depth, complex worldview, and serial narrative structure that formed the cosmology of the so-called quality sitcoms that emerged in the 1970s, often delineated by the troika of *All in the Family* (1971–83), *M*A*S*H* (1972–83), and *The Mary Tyler Moore Show* (1970–77). However, in attempting to provide realistic accounts of family and social life, *The Donna Reed Show* contains progressive, even contradictory, impulses that work to alter the terms of public discourse around gender and the family. The dialogue opened up by *The Donna Reed Show* articulates with its comedic brethren, from the contemporaneous *Dick Van Dyke Show* to the contemporary *Modern Family.*

Donna Stone Meets Laura Petrie

Although Donna Stone remained ensconced in the cultural context of the 1950s and early 1960s, her character exhibited an unusual degree of independence. In some episodes, she could be seen at the wheel of the family car, an image that was quite unusual for sitcom women—and especially housewives—even in the 1960s. The shot of Mary Richards driving her own car in the opening credits of *The Mary Tyler Moore Show* was considered quite progressive in 1970, although Donna Stone had done it first. In many ways, Donna Stone prefigured the more liberated sitcom women who came after *The Donna Reed Show,* whether Laura Petrie in *The Dick Van Dyke Show,* Mary Richards of *The Mary Tyler Moore Show* (with a show also named after the main character), or even the matriarchal *Roseanne.*

While *The Dick Van Dyke Show,* which aired on CBS from 1961 to 1966, is often cited as one of the first liberal Kennedy-era sitcoms, in many ways Laura Petrie is no more modern or independent than Donna Stone. Although *The Donna Reed Show* began three years earlier, both ran until 1966 and shared many similar themes. In fact, in 1961 both shows feature episodes in which Donna Stone and Laura Petrie, at the goading of a friend, dye their hair blonde to become more attractive to their husbands ("Mouse at Play" and "My Blonde-Haired Brunette," respectively). Each immediately regrets her decision and attempts to hide her new hair in fear of her husband's reaction. In "My Blonde-Haired Brunette," Rob learns of Laura's actions in a way that showcases Mary Tyler Moore's comedic talent. She emerges from the bathroom with her hair half blonde and half brunette and breaks down as she tries to explain herself, while in "Mouse at Play," Donna slips out the door and returns to the hairdresser without Alex ever learning of the incident. ("Mouse at Play" does, however, highlight the comedic talents of John Astin as a loony hairdresser and Cloris Leachman as Donna's more progressive friend.) Laura Petrie babbles in Rob's arms, while Donna Stone smoothly handles the situation, albeit through evasion. Both episodes end with a subtle pitch for hair dying, which was becoming fashionable in the early 1960s. Son Richie tells Rob that he preferred Laura as a blonde because she looked prettier, although he adds that he doesn't want his mother to look so pretty. Similarly, Alex observes to Donna that

119

her friend looks attractive with her dyed hair and ironically asks Donna if she would like to try a different hair color.

Donna Stone had a career as a nurse before she married, while Laura Petrie was portrayed as a dancer before her marriage, but both women abandoned their professions to become housewives. In "To Tell or Not to Tell," for example, producer Alan Brady offers Laura a job as a dancer on his show.[1] Her husband Rob's coworker Buddy calls upon Rob to exert his authority and forbid Laura to do it ("You'll be eating frozen dinners," Buddy warns), but Rob decides to let her make her own decision. Predictably, she declares that she would rather be Rob's wife than pursue a career, much as Donna Stone decides to forego a political career in order to take care of Alex and the family in "A Woman's Place." Just as Donna Stone wears the pants in the family and teaches Jeff how to defend himself in "Pardon My Gloves," Laura Petrie proves more adept at self-defense than Rob in the episode "My Mother Can Beat Up My Father." She uses judo on a man who harasses them in a bar, which threatens Rob's masculinity when the story is reported in the paper. There is one major difference that indicates a less patriarchal representation of the sitcom husband in *The Dick Van Dyke Show*. Donna Stone eventually capitulates to Alex's superior boxing skills, but Rob Petrie remains emasculated. He eventually lands in the hospital when he tries to best Laura at judo. The battle of the sexes is a running theme throughout both series, but while Donna Stone often wins through subterfuge and women's wiles, Laura Petrie outright wins.

Like Donna Stone, Laura Petrie pursues interests outside of the house, although her interests are more cultural than community oriented: she takes art classes, visits museums, and even appears on television in one episode. Unlike Donna Stone, Laura is not one to stage public protests, run for political office, or manage a charitable campaign. Donna Stone's public life, underdeveloped as it was, provides a model for women who wanted their voices to be heard, whether in small com-

Donna Stone and Laura Petrie both dye their hair blonde in different episodes of *The Donna Reed* and *Dick Van Dyke Show.*

munities or the larger women's movement. But despite Donna Stone's more public face, Laura Petrie is less tied to the ideology of domestic containment. She is not typically seen housecleaning, and unlike Donna Stone who remains devoted to her children, Laura's life does not revolve around her only child (who is rarely the subject of episodes). Laura Petrie is notable as one of the first sitcom wives to wear form-fitting Capri pants on screen, although Donna Stone also wears pants and high heels in several episodes. While both series went off the air in 1966, Laura Petrie, who dresses fashionably and lives in a modern split-level house just outside Manhattan, is generally considered the chic television wife, while Donna Stone remains the perfect television mother.

The Stones Meet the Munsters

In "What Price Home?"—the penultimate episode of the final season of *The Donna Reed Show*—the Stones offer to sell their house, but ultimately they decide to stay put after all. The episode allows them to reminiscence about the past eight years, from the first episodes when they were newcomers to Hilldale to the last when they were ensconced in the community. In an intertextual nod to another ABC television show (which also went off the air in 1966), Donna shows Trisha a picture of a potential new house, and she rejects it because "It looks like *The Addams Family* house." The Stones' warm cozy suburban home could not be more opposite than *The Addams Family* mansion, just as the two programs, one about suburban insiders and the other about those who do not fit in, are quite different programs.

The strange-family sitcoms of the 1960s such as *The Addams Family* and *The Munsters,* which aired from 1964 to 1966, extended the cultural critique that was hinted at by the trouble in the text of the more familiar domestic families of suburbia.

These shows parody the conventions of the domestic sitcom by inverting the normalcy of its representations. We can see this in the season 1 opening credits of *The Munsters,* which pay homage to those of *The Donna Reed Show. The Donna Reed Show* opens with a perfectly coifed Donna who answers the telephone at the bottom of the stairs (it is for Alex, not her) and then prepares each family member for their day. In *The Munsters,* the monstrous Lily Munster ministers to her family as they, like the Stone family, walk out the door one by one. No phone rings to connect them to the outside world. Their macabre mansion is dark and shadowy, in contrast to the brightly lit Stone home. Unlike the demure Donna Stone who is preoccupied with her familial tasks, Lily Munster poses seductively in front of the camera and plays with her hair as the show opens. Instead of the pleasant but bland "Happy Days" theme song that introduces *The Donna Reed Show,* we hear organ and tuba music, and title and credits for *The Munsters* are introduced with gothic-style lettering that signifies a horror film rather than a television sitcom. While Donna Stone bustles about gathering the family's belongings, Lily Munster holds her ground at the bottom of the stairs as each family member approaches her. She presents her hand to Grandpa, a vampire who tries to bite it rather than kiss it. Niece Marilyn (the normal member of the family) kisses Lily goodbye, and Lily hands a lunchbox to werewolf son Eddie. Finally husband Herman, a Frankenstein-like monster, emerges from an opening below the stairs. Lily offers him her cheek, and he kisses her goodbye, laughing gleefully as he enters the world outside. Both Donna Stone and Lily Munster remain in the home, but Lily Munster does not sigh contentedly once her family is out the door.

Moreover, rather than the uniformity that the 1950s' sitcoms represented, the family portrayed in *The Munsters* signals difference. By bringing otherness into the suburbs, the show calls the normal middle-class television family into question.

According to Spigel (1991, 216), shows such as *The Munsters* "retained the conventions of the previous form, but they made those conventions strange by mismatching form and content." Whereas form and content resonated in a Hollywood sitcom such as *The Donna Reed Show,* in *The Munsters* they contrast with one another, pointing to the strangeness of both the Munster family and the ordinary suburban family they appear to emulate. They were an extended family rather than a nuclear family and were vaguely ethnic, and most importantly, they were monsters whose very existence questioned the image of conformity and normalcy that was promoted, at least on the surface, by *The Donna Reed Show. The Munsters'* difference from the domestic sitcom and its subtle recognition that it shared a certain kinship with *The Donna Reed Show* is indicated in "Operation Herman," in which Lily tells Herman that it is his job to have a father-son talk with Eddie. When Herman protests, Lily points out, "A thing like that is up to the father. Anyone who's watched *Father Knows Best* for nine years knows that." Herman responds, "All right. But Donna Reed always handles these things on her show, you know."

By inverting the conventions of the sitcom genre, *The Munsters* made the familiar strange, and by continuing to evoke the model of the nuclear family, the strange became oddly familiar. Although *The Munsters* and the similar *Addams Family* only lasted two years (they did not survive the transition to color), other strange family sitcoms, such as *My Favorite Martian* (1963–66), *Bewitched* (1964–72), and *I Dream of Jeannie* (1965–70), supplanted the domestic sitcom. These relied more on special effects than a Hollywood cinematic aesthetic, and while they did not feature "monsters," their focus shifted away from the nuclear family. It wasn't until 1984 that *The Cosby Show,* which featured another pediatrician with an office in the house, returned the traditional domestic family sitcom to television.

Roseanne versus *The Donna Reed Show*

Roseanne (1988–97), like the strange family sitcoms of the 1960s, both affirmed and parodied the conventions of the domestic sitcom. But comedian Roseanne Barr developed the series in order to show the other side of the idealized images of the nuclear family on television, especially as portrayed by the then-popular *Cosby Show*. Like Donna Reed, Roseanne Barr was one of the few women on television to have creative control of her own series—she was producer, writer, and star—and was the first woman since Gertrude Berg (and Lucille Ball, in the years following *I Love Lucy*) not to mask her power behind her husband's production company. Whereas Donna Reed was careful to work within the dominant paradigm, Roseanne Barr set out to overtly critique the ideology of "perfect wife and mother" (Karlyn 1995, 260). The figure of Roseanne Conner was the antithesis of the 1950s' domestic sitcom mom: she was overweight, loud, and domineering, while her family was beset by financial hardships and emotional pain. In presenting working-class life, the show included topics such as mental illness, gay relationships, domestic abuse, unemployment, and alcoholism and also addressed controversial issues involving the children, such as masturbation, birth control, leaving home, and teen pregnancy.

Season 7's "The Clip Show" directly addresses the disparity between *Roseanne* and traditional domestic sitcoms such as *The Donna Reed Show*. In this reflexive episode, the actresses who play the sitcom mothers from *Leave It to Beaver, Lassie* (1954–74), *Please Don't Eat the Daisies* (1965–67), *The Jeffersons* (1975–85), and *The Wonder Years* (1988–93) visit Roseanne. They are appalled when clips from past episodes show her engaged in activities such as smoking pot, dressing as a man, taking DJ's birthday money, and kissing a woman. Roseanne directly challenges the patriarchal vantage of traditional sitcoms: One of the sitcom moms asks, "You mean you're the boss in your own family?" Roseanne replies, "Yep, and I get all the good jokes too." Later she adds, "Well, see, nobody upstages me. That's why they call the show *Roseanne*." She concludes the conversation with "Well, the important thing is that on my show, I'm the boss and father knows squat." Whereas the same could be said for Donna Reed, her authority was far more muted. Donna Stone did not challenge norms of femininity or middle-class propriety that was *Roseanne*'s raison d'être. *The Donna Reed Show* sows the seeds of critique, while *Roseanne* bears their fruit.

The *Roseanne* episode "Sweet Dreams," in comparison to "Three Part Mother" in *The Donna Reed Show*, highlights the inverted relationship between the two shows. In "Three Part Mother," discussed in chapter 2, Donna is besieged by her family's requests that she be in three places at the same time. She is angry and resentful and escapes to bed, but she relents when they apologize and even manages to accomplish the seemingly impossible task of giving everyone a little piece of her: she makes it to each event just in time. At day's end, she smiles contentedly as she drifts off to sleep and hears the family's voices calling her. They have colonized her unconscious, apparently erasing the rancor that has shaped the narrative. She appears to be the self-sacrificing wife and mother whose needs are subordinated to her family.

In "Sweet Dreams," Roseanne is similarly under siege by her family. She wants to take a bath alone, but Dan is working on the plumbing, and the kids are all using the bathroom for various reasons. While she is waiting she falls asleep, and the episode shifts into a dream sequence. Her bathroom has become an opulent Roman spa, and two muscular, scantily clad men pamper her. But her idyll is interrupted when each member of her family continues to prevent her from taking her bath. Donna Stone's solution to her family's unreasonable demands is to take a time-out, and her resistance dissipates as soon as they apologize. In Roseanne's dream, however, her solution is to murder each of them. She is put on trial, essentially for having desires that contradict the ideology of the self-sacrificing mother: seeking pleasure for herself rather than achieved through the accomplishments of her family. "All I wanted was ten minutes alone in my own bathroom!" she protests. Even when the children apologize, she is not transformed. The problem is only resolved when the dream shifts from the courtroom to a musical. Her friend Vonda sings "Ain't Misbehaving" in her defense, and everyone in the courtroom begins to sing and dance, ending with a resounding "We love Roseanne." Roseanne also belts out a song whose lyrics verbalize the drudgery of the housewife: "a load of laundry, a load of working, a load of shopping, do it please, do it now, do it mom, do it Rose, do it right do it good, do it fast." As she continues to sing, there is a superimposition of images of her family, reminiscent of the voices at the end of "Three Part Mother." But these images do not satisfy Roseanne; instead they reinforce her problem, and the images of her family eventually disappear as the camera shifts to a dissolve. In "Three Part Mother," Donna is triumphant when she manages to be in three places at once, and by the end of the episode all of her frustrations seemingly disappear. When Roseanne awakes, however, the family returns with their demands. She tells Dan that she had a strange dream, and he jests, "You're back in Kansas now. And there's no place like home." Roseanne enters the bathroom, finally getting her coveted bath. "Yeah, bull," she retorts, getting the final word. The episode concludes with a dissolve to Roseanne's family and friends, once again assembled in the courtroom and repeating the chorus "We love Roseanne." The overhead camera zooms in to a close-up of Roseanne in the middle of the group, smiling and holding her arms out to the camera. But there is no tidy resolution here. Roseanne is only satisfied in her fantasy: the musical in which everyone expresses love for her. The dissatisfactions that mark her real life are not disavowed, as they are in "Three Part Mother."

Traditional Families to *Modern Family*

Contemporary sitcoms continue the dialogue with *The Donna Reed Show.* Whereas *Roseanne* attempted to invert the conventions of the domestic sitcom (while maintaining its commitment to the nuclear family), *Modern Family* maintains the sentimentality of Donna Reed while providing an ironic edge. *The Donna Reed Show* and even *Roseanne* took the concept of the nuclear family as a given, while *Modern Family* negotiates what family means in the contemporary world. The show assumes diversity, with its ensemble cast that includes two gay parents and a biracial May–December marriage, along with a more traditional, if somewhat dysfunctional, nuclear family. Even its form develops the genre. Like *The Donna Reed Show, Modern Family* is a single-camera sitcom, although without a laugh track, and its humor relies more on characters and situations than on comedic repartee. The show mimics reality television by using a mock documentary style whereby characters directly address the camera to provide their insights, a contemporary touch that creates humor by magnifying the divide between reality and perception. The result is a self-aware sitcom that plays with sitcom stereotypes and conventions.

Season 1's "Moon Landing" episode of *Modern Family* is a contemporary take on the "Career Woman" episode of *The Donna Reed Show* (discussed in chapter 3). Both Donna Stone and Claire Dunphy are housewives who gave up careers to stay home with their families, and both episodes deal with their encounter with an old friend who has chosen career over work. In both, well-known film actresses play the accomplished friend: Esther Williams in "Career Woman" and Minnie Driver in "Moon Landing." The point of "Career Woman" is to pull Donna's friend Molly out of the world of work and into the bosom of the nuclear family. She is a successful, sophisticated fashion designer and is fearful of what she will sacrifice if she decides to marry a small-town doctor. As they converse, Donna insists that she is content with her life, her assertion reinforced by the backdrop of the cozy living room and the fire in the hearth. But it is the children, rather than the lifestyle, that seem to sway Molly. She is enamored when she meets Mary and Jeff and exclaims to Donna, "And I thought I was accomplishing something all this time. Oh, Donna, you have so much." When the kids kiss Donna goodnight, Molly comments, "Now that part of the routine I could like." Later, she takes Mary shopping and allows the shopkeeper to mistake her for Mary's mother. The joys of motherhood trump her glamorous career, and she decides to marry the doctor. This resolution is not uncomplicated, and Molly's quite valid reservations have been expressed throughout the episode, but the narrative lesson is to reaffirm marriage.

In *Modern Family*, Claire's friend Valerie comes to visit. Valerie and Claire once worked together, although Claire quit to get married. (The dialogue indicates that she gave birth to daughter Haley four months later.) When Claire and Valerie meet, Valerie squeezes Claire's ring finger as she asks what it is like to have chosen motherhood, which prompts Claire, in a direct address to the camera, to conclude that Valerie is jealous of her life. "She was looking at my life as something that she wanted but never had," Claire observes. This is the conventional stereotype of the single woman who really just wants home and family that was affirmed in "Career Woman," but here it is challenged. Valerie then tells Claire that she is now a top executive. "If you hadn't left, it probably would have been you," she disingenuously remarks. When Claire asks her if she has a serious relationship, Valerie replies that she has four lovers in different cities around the world. There is no indication here that she secretly wants to settle into a monogamous relationship. Valerie is waiting for a phone call about a promotion, and again in a direct address to the camera Claire admits that she is jealous that Valerie would get the most coveted job in the company. Valerie gets the call but at first doesn't tell Claire that she did indeed get the job.

Claire then remarks on camera, "That's when it hit me. She wasn't jealous of me. She pitied me. And part of me wanted to take her back to my house and show her everything she was missing in her sad, childless, husbandless life." This is the lesson of "Career Woman," and the conventional ending would have Valerie realizing the joys of parenthood. Instead Valerie visits the Dunphy home, where everything is in disarray. Haley and her boyfriend Dylan are first fighting and then are engaged in a passionate embrace in the hallway, a rat has escaped from a carton of recyclable bottles that Alex and Luke have brought home, Luke is wearing only underwear after having spilled one of the bottles that has also drenched the carpet with alcohol, and Dylan's car has blocked Phil into a porta-potty. Valerie cannot leave quickly enough to escape the domestic mayhem. She is not moved to change her life, and she does not secretly desire domesticity. The show does not affirm that a particular way of life is better but only affirms that they are different. In the end Claire, after departing in a rage, returns home in the midst of the family dinner, and Phil simply pulls out a seat for her. The family continues their conversation, with Claire now in her place. She is grateful, and the sequence ends with Claire voicing her love for her family on camera. "Moon Landing" ends with a reaffirmation of the family but unlike "Career Woman" allows for difference.

From Donna Stone to Donna Reed

In many ways, Donna Stone was the alter ego of Donna Reed, a relationship fostered by the Screen Gems publicity machine that worked to merge Donna Reed and Donna Stone in the public mind. Donna Reed/Stone did commercials for Campbell's Soup and Singer sewing machines, and Donna Reed provided advice on family and parenting in popular magazines. Indeed, the show deliberately encouraged the blurring of the identities of Donna Reed and Donna Stone by giving Donna

Stone the same maiden name and biography as Donna Reed. Dream sequences almost always entailed iconic femme fatale film roles that evoked Donna Reed as film star. Donna Reed also used the show to reflect her own life. She always said that the show should reflect the way real-life families behave, and many of the show's themes and issues were drawn from her own experiences as a mother and as a working woman facing the conflicting demands of her family.

While it is instructive to look at the traces of Donna Reed in Donna Stone, it is also useful to consider Donna Reed's later trajectory as a manifestation of the public imagination of Donna Stone in the tumultuous 1960s. The landmark events that marked the 1960s are well known, beginning with the assassination of President Kennedy in 1963. U.S. involvement in Vietnam led to protests against what was perceived as an unjust war. Marginalized groups that had initially begun to mobilize in the 1950s—the women's rights, civil rights, and gay rights movements—gained momentum and took their protests to the streets.

Donna Reed benefited from the women's movement that led many women to make changes in their lives. For years, she had promulgated the image of Donna Stone as perfect wife and mother. Once freed from this responsibility and no longer connected by *The Donna Reed Show,* in 1970 Reed divorced Tony Owen. (She married Grover Asmus, a retired army colonel, in 1974.) She became a vocal critic of the way the film and television industries treated women and took few acting roles after the show went off the air. By way of explanation, she asserted that "I didn't work because I didn't get the kind of scripts I wanted. I didn't want to play helpless women and victims" (Royce 1990, 10). She also denounced male producers and directors for the overabundance of "neurotic, sick, and amoral female characters" as well as "the scarcity of secure, strong-willed career women" (11).

While Donna Stone was an emerging activist, Donna Reed followed through. She became chairwoman of Direct Relief International in 1965, an organization that provides medical equipment and supplies to needy areas worldwide. In 1967 she became a cofounder, along with writer Barbara Avedon, of the anti–Vietnam War group Another Mother for Peace. According to Shelley Fabares, many people were appalled that the woman known as the "perfect mom" was publically taking a stand against the war (Fabares 1998). The woman who was the idealized cultural icon of the 1950s' mother became a 1960s' social protestor. Donna Reed campaigned for Eugene McCarthy, attended the 1968 Democratic National Convention, went to rallies, and did extensive research into oil repositories off the coast of Vietnam, after which she published an article with coauthor Dorothy Jones in the Another Mother for Peace newsletter. As a result, thousands of women wrote to Washington, D.C., to urge that hearings be conducted, and Donna Reed went to Washington and confronted Henry Kissinger. Later, she worked with Ralph Nader to advocate for safer nuclear power plants. Donna Reed's public career was in many ways a credible imagined path for the assertive though fictional Donna Stone.

Donna Reed returned to television in the late 1970s with several guest appearances on dramatic series and in 1984 an ill-fated turn as Ellie Ewing on *Dallas*. She was replacing Barbara Bel Geddes who was ill, and when Bel Geddes announced that she would return, Reed was fired. She filed a lawsuit for violation of contract, which Lorimar settled with her. A year later, in 1985, she was diagnosed with pancreatic cancer, and she died three months later.

The Donna Reed Show aired for many years in syndication, which means that it was still remembered long after it went off the air, even if popular memories were more tied to what people thought the show represented rather than to its actual content. Initially Screen Gems and then Columbia Pictures Television were responsible for syndicating the show. In 1985 the show provided the inspiration for Nickelodeon's Nick at Nite. Lore has it that when branding consultants were presented with two hundred episodes of *The Donna Reed Show*, they came up with the idea of the first oldies television network ("Nick at Nite" n.d.). As a result, *The Donna Reed Show*, along with other classic television shows, ran on Nick at Nite from 1985 to 1994. The strategy was to surround classic programming with innovative promotions, such as a short clip that defined "Donna-holism" as a compulsive need to watch *The Donna Reed Show* or a tribute to Mother's Day that featured a weeklong marathon of episodes. In 2003, the forty-year distribution agreement between Columbia Pictures and *The Donna Reed Show* expired, and copyright reverted to Donna Reed's heirs. As of this writing, the first four seasons have been released on DVD.

In 1987 Donna Reed's husband Grover Asmus, the actress Shelley Fabares, and various friends and relatives founded the Donna Reed Foundation for the Performing Arts. It is a nonprofit organization based in Reed's hometown of Denison, Iowa, and is dedicated to memorializing Donna Reed and honoring her commitment to the performing arts. The foundation provides scholarships for young performers, workshops by industry professionals, and cultural events such as plays, concerts, and film series. In 2004 the foundation opened the Donna Reed Heritage Museum to preserve the memory of Donna Reed.

Still, the cultural image of Donna Reed remains that of perfect wife and mother, and *The Donna Reed Show* is still often compared to other domestic sitcoms such as *The Adventures of Ozzie and Harriet, Leave It to Beaver,* and *Father Knows Best.* Yet *The Donna Reed Show* is more of a milestone than its television cohorts. Reed was one of the first major film stars to move to television and one of the few women in early television to have behind-the-scenes control of her program. Because of Reed's background in film, many of the writers and directors came from Hollywood, and the show was an early example of a television program that had a cinematic aesthetic and sensibility. Many episodes pushed the envelope in terms of both style and content; especially in later seasons, the show occasionally addressed social issues that were not typically seen in situation comedies. More importantly, the character of Donna Stone managed to both conform to and alter television representations of the housewife and in so doing provided a transition to the more liberated women of the 1960s and 1970s.

Hopefully as more viewers visit *The Donna Reed Show* on DVD, it will earn its place in television history. A close viewing of *The Donna Reed Show* makes apparent that it was not as idealized a vision of the patriarchal nuclear family as it first appeared. Yet the saccharine image of Donna Reed lives on. In a famous 2001 episode of *The Gilmore Girls* titled "That Damn Donna Reed," Lorelai, her daughter Rory, and Rory's boyfriend Dean are watching reruns of *The Donna Reed Show* and are shocked that Dean is unfamiliar with Donna Reed.

> Lorelai: You don't know who Donna Reed is? The quintessential 50s' mom with the perfect 50s' family?
> Rory: Never without a smile and high heels.
> Lorelai: Hair that if you hit it with a hammer, it would crack?
> Dean: So, it's a show?
> Rory: It's a lifestyle.
> Lorelai: It's a religion.

Such is the legacy of *The Donna Reed Show*.

Introduction

1. See *Cheers,* "A Diminished Rebecca with a Diminished Cliff" (1992); *The Nanny,* "Here Comes the Brood" (1993); and *The Gilmore Girls,* "That Damn Donna Reed" (2001).

2. Fultz (1998) notes Reed's role as producer in his biography *In Search of Donna Reed.* Reed's role as producer is also confirmed in various published interviews with Shelley Fabares, Paul Petersen, and Reed's daughter Mary Owen.

3. See Spigel (1991) and Metz (2007).

4. Spigel notes that her calculation refers to sitcoms that revolved around domestic situations. She does not include sitcoms that focused on working life rather than families (such as *The Many Loves of Dobie Gillis*), were set in urban areas (such as *The Danny Thomas Show*), or were set in rural areas (such as *The Andy Griffith Show*).

5. See Weinblatt (1994).

Chapter 1

1. Loretta Young was also a film actress who produced and starred in *The Loretta Young Show* (1953–61). However, this was a dramatic anthology series rather than a family comedy, and thus I do not include Loretta Young as having a direct influence on Donna Reed.

Chapter 2

1. Multicamera sitcoms filmed in front of a live audience reemerged

in the 1970–71 season with *The Mary Tyler Moore Show, All in the Family,* and *The Odd Couple,* the latter of which switched from a single camera to a multicamera format shot before a live audience in its second season.

2. In *Family Plots: The De-Oedipalization of Popular Culture,* Heller (1995) discusses this episode from a psychoanalytic point of view.

3. As Heller (1995, 53) notes, he "is not the first fictional doctor to recommend mastery over women through the administration of drugs."

4. Leibman (1995) also relies on the work of Peter Brooks, John G. Cawelti, and Thomas Elsaesser on the melodrama. See Peter Brooks, *The Melodramatic Imagination: Balzac, Henry James, Melodrama, and the Mode of Excess* (New York: Columbia University Press, 1985); John G. Cawelti, *Adventure, Mystery, and Romance: Formula Stories as Art and Pop Culture* (Chicago: University of Chicago Press, 1976); and Thomas Elsaesser, "Tales of Sound and Fury: Observations on the Family Melodrama," in *Home Is Where the Heart Is: Studies in Melodrama,* edited by Christine Gledhill 43–69 (London: British Film Institute, 1987).

Chapter 5

1. For a discussion of this episode, see Marc (1989, 114).

REFERENCES

137

Althusser, Louis. 2005. *For Marx.* London: Verso.

Anderson, Christopher. 1994. *Hollywood TV: The Studio System in the Fifties.* Austin: University of Texas Press.

Anderson, Nancy. 1965. "Why Donna Reed Is So Worried about Paul Petersen's Bachelor Parties." *Screenland,* October.

Barker, David. 1985. "Production Techniques as Communication." Critical Studies in Mass Communication, 234–46.

Boddy, William. 1993. *Fifties Television: The Industry and Its Critics.* Chicago: University of Illinois Press.

Breines, Wini. 1992. *Young, White, and Miserable: Growing Up Female in the Fifties.* Chicago: University of Chicago Press.

Bronson, Fred. 2003. *The Billboard Book of Number 1 Hits.* 5th ed. New York: Billboard Books.

Caldwell, John Thornton. 1995. *Televisuality: Style, Crisis and Authority in American Television.* New Brunswick, NJ: Rutgers University Press.

Castleman, Harry, and Walter J. Podrazik. 1984. *Watching TV: Six Decades of American Television.* 2nd ed. New York: Syracuse University Press.

Christy, George. 1960. "It's Worth Fighting to Save a Marriage" *Photoplay,* February, pp. 55, 71–73.

Dern, Marian. 1963. "Donna Reed: Sweet-Sincere-Solvent." *TV Guide,* June 20–26, pp. 10–13.

Doane, Mary Ann. 1982. "Film and the Masquerade: Theorizing the Female Spectator." *Screen* 23: 74–87.

Donna Reed Foundation for the Performing Arts. n.d. "The Donna Reed

Show." http://www.donnareed.org/html/templates/dr_detail.php?dr_detail=drshw.

Donna Reed Quotes. n.d. http://thinkexist.com/quotes/donna_reed/.

Douglas, Susan J. 1994. *Where the Girls Are: Growing Up Female with the Mass Media.* New York: Random House.

Edgerton, Gary R. 2007. *The Columbia History of American Television.* New York: Columbia University Press.

Ellis, John. 2000. *Seeing Things: Television in the Age of Uncertainty.* London: I. B. Tauris.

Fabares, Shelley. 1998. Interview. "Donna Reed: I'll Take the Moon." DVD. Directed by Patty Ivins Specht. A&E Biography Series.

Fiedler, Leslie. 1960. *Love and Death in the American Novel.* Champaign, IL: Dalkey Archive.

Field, Eunice. 1963. "Donna Reed: My Story Is Not for Children—or Prudes." *TV Radio Mirror,* September.

French, Philip. 2010. "Philip French's Screen Legends." *Observer,* January 10, p. 14. www.guardian.co.uk/film/2010/jan/10/screen-legend-donna-reed.

Freud, Sigmund. 1960. *Jokes and Their Relation to the Unconscious.* Translated by James Strachey. New York: Norton.

Fultz, Jay. 1998. *In Search of Donna Reed.* Iowa City: University of Iowa Press.

Gitlin, Todd. 1983. *Inside Prime Time.* New York: Pantheon.

Greene, Doyle. 2008. *Politics and the American Television Comedy: A Critical Survey from I Love Lucy to South Park.* Jefferson, NC: McFarland.

Gregory, James. 1964. "Donna Reed: What Every Girl Should Know." *TV Picture Life,* July.

Grimes, Wallace A. 1960. "Stay Home Girls! How Girls Can Break into TV." *Minnesota TV Times,* August 20–26.

Hamamoto, Darrell. 1989. *Nervous Laughter: Television Situation Comedy and Liberal Democratic Ideology.* New York: Praeger.

Haralovich, Mary Beth. 2003. "Sitcoms and Suburbs: Positioning the Fifties Homemaker." In *Critiquing the Sitcom: A Reader,* edited by Joanne Morreale, 69–85. New York: Syracuse University Press.

Heath, Steven. 1986. "Joan Riviere and the Masquerade." In *Formations of Fantasy,* edited by Victor Burgin, James Donald, and Cora Kaplan, 45–61. London: Methuen.

Heller, Dana. 1995. *Family Plots: The De-Oedipalization of Popular Culture.* Philadelphia: University of Pennsylvania Press.

Jenkins, Henry. n.d. "'The All American Handful': Dennis the Menace, Permissive Childrearing, and the Bad Boy Tradition." http://web.mit.edu/cms/People/henry3/dennis.html.

Jones, Gerard. 1992. *Honey I'm Home: Sitcoms Selling the American Dream.* New York: St. Martin's.

"Just What the Doctor Ordered." 1958. *TV Guide,* December 13, pp. 9–11.

Karlyn, Kathleen Rowe. 1995. "Roseanne: Unruly Woman as Domestic Goddess." In *Critiquing the Sitcom,* edited by Joanne Morreale, 251–61. New York: SUNY University Press.

Landay, Lori. 2010. *I Love Lucy.* Detroit: Wayne State University Press.

Leibman, Nina C. 1988. "Leave Mother Out: The Fifties Family in American Film and Television." *Wide Angle* 10: 24–41.

———. 1995. *Living Room Lectures: The Fifties Family in Film and Television.* Austin: University of Texas Press.

Lewis, Amy. 1964. "Donna Reed: She Puts the Family First." *Screenland,* May, pp. 42–44, 48–49.

Lipsitz, George. 1986. "The Meaning of Memory: Family, Class, and Ethnicity in Early Network Television." *Cultural Anthropology* 1, no. 4 (November): 79–116.

———. 1990. *Time Passages: Collective Memory and American Popular Culture.* Minneapolis: University of Minnesota Press.

Marc, David. 1989. *Comic Visions: Television Comedy and American Culture.* New York: Unwin Hyman.

May, Elaine Tyler. 1999. *Homeward Bound: American Families in the Postwar Period.* New York: Basic Books.

Mellencamp, Patricia. 1986. "Situation Comedy, Feminism, and Freud: Discourses of Gracie and Lucy." In *Studies in Entertainment: Critical Approaches to Mass Culture,* edited by Tania Modelski, 80–95. Bloomington: Indiana University Press.

Metz, Walter. 2007. *Bewitched.* Detroit: Wayne State University Press.

"Never Argue with a Woman: As Donna Reed Has Proved, It Seldom Pays." 1959. *TV Guide,* August 8, pp. 9–11.

"Nick at Nite." n.d. Wikipedia. http://en.wikipedia.org/wiki/Nick_at_Nite.

Petersen, Paul. 2008. "Paul Petersen and Mary Owen Q & A." *The Donna Reed Show Season One.* DVD. Produced by Thomas J. O'Connor. Arts Alliance America.

Plath, James. 2008. "Behind the Scenes of The Donna Reed Show: A Conversation with Paul Petersen." http://www.dvdtown.com/news/behind-the-scenes-of-the-donna-reed-show-a-conversation-with-paul-petersen/6073/.

139

Riviere, Joan. (1929) 1986. "Womanliness as a Masquerade." In *Formations of Fantasy,* edited by Victor Burgin, James Donald, and Cora Kaplan, 35–44. London: Methuen. Originally published as "Womanliness as a Masquerade," *International Journal of Psychoanalysis* 10 (1929): 303–13.

Royce, Brenda Scott. 1990. *Donna Reed: A Bio-Bibliography.* New York: Greenwood.

Schrum, Kelly. 2004. *They Wore Bobby Sox: The Emergence of Teen Girl's Culture, 1920–1945.* New York: Palgrave Macmillan.

Seaton, Maureen. 2010. "When I Was *The Donna Reed Show.*" *Missouri Review* 33, no. 3 (Fall): 117.

Silverman, Kaja. 1988. *The Acoustic Mirror: The Female Voice in Psychoanalysis and Cinema.* Bloomington: Indiana University Press.

Smith, Glen D. 2007. *Something on My Own: Gertrude Berg and American Broadcasting.* New York: Syracuse University Press.

Spigel, Lynn. 1991. "From Domestic Space to Outer Space: The 1960s Fantastic Family Sitcom." In *Close Encounters: Film, Feminism, and Science Fiction,* edited by Constance Penley, Elisabeth Lyon, Lynn Spigel, and Janet Bergstrom, 205–36. Minneapolis: University of Minnesota Press.

———. 1992. *Make Room for TV: Television and the Family Ideal in Postwar America.* Chicago: University of Chicago Press.

———. 2001. *Welcome to the Dreamhouse: Popular Media and Postwar Suburbs.* Durham, NC: Duke University Press.

"The Farmer's Daughter Who Went to Town." 1961. *TV Guide,* May 6–12, pp. 12–15.

Timberg, Bernard. n.d. "Gertrude Berg, 'Yoo-Hoo, Mrs. Goldberg,' and the Re-Discovery of a Television Auteur." Flowtv.org. http://flowtv.org/2009/06/gertrude-berg-yoo-hoo-mrs-goldberg-and-the-re-discovery-of-a-television-auteurbernard-m-timberg-university-of-north-carolina-chapel-hill/.

Tucker, David C. 2007. *The Women Who Made Television Funny: Ten Stars of 1950s Sitcoms.* Jefferson, NC: McFarland.

Watson, Mary Ann. 2008. *Defining Visions: Television and the American Experience in the 20th Century.* Malden, MA: Blackwell.

Weinblatt, Tinky "Dakota." 1994. "What Ozzie Did for a Living." *Velvet Light Trap* 33 (Spring): 14–23.

Wells, Paul. 1998. "Where Everybody Knows Your Name: Open Convictions and Closed Contexts in American Situation Comedy." In *Because*

I Tell a Joke or Two: Comedy, Politics, and Social Difference, edited by
Steven Wagg, 180–201. New York: Routledge.
"Wheeling and Dealing, Hollywood Style." 1962. *TV Guide,* July 20–21,
21–27.

References

150

151